Hello, TOMORROW!

CINDY TRIMM

CHARISMA
HOUSE

HELLO, TOMORROW! by Cindy Trimm
Published by Charisma House
Charisma Media/Charisma House Book Group
600 Rinehart Road
Lake Mary, Florida 32746
www.charismahouse.com

Visit the author's website at www.trimminternational.com.

Library of Congress Cataloging-in-Publication Data:
An application to register this book for cataloging has been submitted to the Library of Congress.
International Standard Book Number: 978-1-62999-549-6
E-book ISBN: 978-1-62999-550-2

This publication is translated in Spanish under the title *¡Hola, mañana!*, copyright © 2018 by Cindy Trimm, published by Casa Creación, a Charisma Media company. All rights reserved.

18 19 20 21 22 — 987654321
Printed in the United States of America

CONTENTS

— ◆ ◆ ◆ —

INTRODUCTION

◆ ◆ ◆

For last year's words belong to last year's language
And next year's words await another voice.
—T. S. ELIOT

It SEEMS MY entire life I've been on a mission to empower ordinary people, people like you and me, to find their voice and make it heard in extraordinary ways. In all of my travels across the globe, the one common denominator I see among people everywhere is the need to feel as though they have a voice—a self-determining voice that, if nothing else, puts them in the driver's seat of their own lives. This has also been a common thread throughout all of my books, beginning with the original *Rules of Engagement*.

I've discovered that not only is this need universal; it's as deeply felt today as it has ever been. More than ever, my audiences want to know how to bridge the gap between what is and what can be—between who they are now and who they can ultimately become. They're looking for practical strategies not only to enable them to "press toward the mark for the prize of the high calling of God" (Phil. 3:14, KJV) but also to discern what that high calling is for them. A map and compass can help you get anywhere, but you must first know where you're going.

I want to help you shift your thinking so you are able to see farther afield in the direction of what's possible for you. I want to equip you with the tools you need to launch yourself into the deep of your greatest potential. I want to show you how to tap into your own powerful voice and your imagination to steer the ship of your life—and then how to unfurl the sails of faith to speed yourself on your way to the fulfillment of God-inspired vision.

In *Commanding Your Morning*, I taught in detail about how to harness the power of your thoughts and words to reorder your day and ultimately your life. In *Hello, Tomorrow!*, I want to show you how to harness the power of a compelling vision to change not only your future but ultimately the world. I want to give you a new voice for a new day.

The word *voice* is rooted in the Latin *vocare*, which means to call or invoke.[1] An English understanding of the word lends the meaning "invisible spirit or force that directs or suggests." French adds the sense "report,"[2] while in the *Oxford English Dictionary* we find "an agency by which a particular point of view is expressed or represented," leading to its implication of one's "distinctive tone or style."[3]

Interestingly the word *hello* was originally used as a call to attract attention. It is an alteration of *hallo*, which comes from a fifteenth-century word meaning "a shipman's cry to incite effort." *Hello* gained popularity as a word with the rise of the telephone, and could be considered a word that gives voice to your voice. Incidentally *hello* won out over Alexander Graham Bell's suggestion of using *ahoy* when answering the telephone. I also got a kick out of learning that by the late 1880s telephone operators were known as "hello-girls."[4]

So how do we call to attract or invoke the best that tomorrow has to offer? How do we cross that bridge from where we are today to where we want to be in the tomorrows of the future? How do we navigate the ship of our life closer to the shore of our dreams, where we can call out "Hello!" to our destiny?

We do this with vision. Vision calls you out of your past to participate in your future. It points to cultural transformation, institutional restructuring, systemic change, human progress, political enfranchisement, future potentialities, spiritual realities, and economic possibilities—all of which have the power to change the trajectory of individual lives, corporations, communities, and countries.

This is the transformational power of vision—of being able to see those shores of possibility on the horizon. A vision that pulls you forward enables you to overcome your past and surmount the limitations of your present conditions. But not only do you have to be able to see what's possible in the distance—to be farsighted, so to speak—you must also be able to map out and navigate toward what you see. You must become the Christopher Columbus of your own potential. You must learn to follow your own north star and navigate through life's seas and storms, and like the Magi who were led to Jesus by a star (Matt. 2:1–2), you must be able to read the signs from heaven for clues that will lead you toward a new world of possibilities you have only dreamed of.

With this in mind, I endeavor to take you on a journey using the following symbols as metaphors:

- The ship: your life

- The map: your vision

- The compass: your values

- The north star: your desired direction

- The ship's wheel: your thoughts and imagination

- The sails: your faith

- The rudder: your words

- The wind: your passion

- The shore: your destiny

- The anchor: your fear

- The hull: your mind

- Barnacles on the hull: your negative emotions

As a life strategist, minister, entrepreneur, thought leader, and best-selling author, I am asked every day, and often many times a day, by people in all walks of life the same types of questions: How can I realize my dreams and accomplish my goals? How can I get from point A to point B? How can I find happiness? How can I find meaning and purpose? How can I make a difference in this world? The questions, no matter how worded, are the same.

No one sets out in life to feel unfulfilled. Yet modern life has a way of stressing us out until stress is all we feel. Wake up, hit the alarm, get up, get ready for work, make lunches and pack book bags, drop kids off at school, fight with traffic, make it to the office, where the phones are already ringing, attend mind-numbing meeting after meeting, pick up take-out on the way home, pay bills, and on and on until we fall into bed exhausted way after 11 p.m. Some days, for some people, the stress overshadows everything else. When stress is the only thing you focus on, you experience even more of it—because what we focus on expands.

Instead of focusing on stress, focus on a horizon of unlimited possibilities that stretches out ahead of you. Dare to leave the safe harbor of the familiar and set sail. This book has been written to make certain you have a clearly determined way to navigate the ship of your life—vision. Don't be like the masses who refuse to push away from the shores of safety because they are afraid of possible storms brewing out at sea. Fear is an irrational emotion that cripples you and causes you to remain anchored at the harbor.

People seem to buy up so much emotional insurance against risk that they have little or no strength left to pursue their dreams and accomplish their goals. Life is risky business. I have heard of people walking down the street and breaking their ankles, or driving to work and experiencing a head-on collision, but I still walk down streets and drive. The famous motivational speaker Jim Rohn once said wittily, "Life is risky. Let me tell you how risky it is—you won't make it out alive."[5] He further quips, "If you want something that pulls you through all kinds of challenges and difficulties, you have to have something out there. Beyond today. Beyond next week. Beyond next month. Beyond this year, that pulls you into the future. And the clearer it is, the stronger it pulls."[6] Remember, a ship left in the harbor will eventually corrode and rot because of the corrosive elements of the sea. So staying put is as risky as launching out into the deep. Even on your maiden voyage, there's a risk of meeting a storm or two, but a ship equipped with the sails of faith will be able to make it through.

Even though you stand at the helm, God is ultimately the captain of your ship and your life. Since your captain's resolve will determine whether the ship reaches its destination or turns back to the harbor, you have nothing to worry about. "'For I know the plans and thoughts that I have for you,' says the LORD, 'plans for peace and well-being and not for disaster, to give you a future and a hope'" (Jer. 29:11, AMP). So cast off your fear and make preparations. And when the storms of life come, He will show you what emotional cargo should be thrown overboard to preserve your life.

While contingency plans can help you overcome obstacles, lifeboats are not recommended. Lifeboats are what you use when you believe the ship is going to sink. The same captain who showed you your destination via your vision will help you weather the storm when the rough waters rise and the winds blow. You might be tempted to go for the lifeboat, but God's will is certain, and there is no need to abandon ship.

Benjamin Disraeli said, "I have brought myself, by long meditation, to the conviction that a human being with a settled purpose must accomplish it, and that nothing can resist a will that will stake even existence upon its fulfillment."[7] Simply put, don't quit. Make course corrections as needed so that your ship arrives at its destination at the appointed time.

Here is something else to consider: As the ship gets close to shore, the fog might roll in. Don't panic. Instead, look for the lighthouse. It will be the very thing that will help you avoid sharp rocks and ominous reefs that would cause you to run aground. Your lighthouse is your beacon of hope. Hope is faith's companion. Keep believing because these obstacles will be the last test before you reach your new harbor.

As Dr. Seuss so famously said, "You have brains in your head. You have feet in your shoes. You can steer yourself any direction you choose."[8]

You have places to go and things to do, and I pray the tools and strategies offered in this book will help you get there and accomplish everything you set out to accomplish. Life is not a dress rehearsal, so I pray you live all the days of your life to their fullest, regretting nothing in the process.

Some of you set sail in big ships; you put to sea to do business in faraway ports. Out at sea you saw God in action, saw his breathtaking ways with the ocean: With a word he called up the wind—an ocean storm, towering waves! You shot high in the sky, then the bottom dropped out; your hearts were stuck in your throats. You were spun like a top, you reeled like a drunk, you didn't know which end was up. Then you called out to God in your desperate condition; he got you out in the nick of time. He quieted the wind down to a whisper, put a muzzle on all the big waves. And you were so glad when the storm died down, and he led you safely back to harbor. So thank God for his marvelous love, for his miracle mercy to the children he loves.

—Psalm 107:23–32, The Message

"Listen to this message from the LORD! This is what the LORD says: By this time tomorrow…"
—2 KINGS 7:1, NLT

STEP ONE

Build a Bridge to Your Future

Men go forth to marvel at the heights of mountains
and the huge waves of the sea, the broad flow of the
rivers, the vastness of the ocean, the orbits of the
stars, and yet they neglect to marvel at themselves.
—St. Augustine

You may not be able to see a path right
now, but that doesn't mean it's not there.
—Nick Vujicic

CHAPTER ONE

It's Your Future—Own It!

There is no greater discovery than seeing
God as the author of your destiny.
—Ravi Zacharias

There is surely a future hope for you, and
your hope will not be cut off.
—Proverbs 23:18

THE BIBLE GIVES a two-verse glimpse into the life of a man by the name of Jabez, who saw himself differently than those around him. He recognized that cultural and social limitations were restricting his thinking and asked God to enlarge his coast.

> And Jabez called on the God of Israel, saying, Oh that thou wouldest bless me indeed, and enlarge my coast, and that thine hand might be with me, and that thou wouldest keep me from evil, that it may not grieve me! And God granted him that which he requested.
>
> —1 Chronicles 4:10, KJV

I considered the word *coast* and thought of it as a metaphor for psychological boundaries and self-imposed limitations that restrict us from thinking big and expecting more than what we perceive is possible based on our worldview and the realities of our personal lives. Further, in seeking practical application for this verse, I considered the fact that many people are restricted from progressing in life because of small thinking or feel they are stuck in a particular station in life because of circumstances beyond their control. People struggling to get a break in life or facing discouraging or desperate moments need God to divinely enlarge their intellectual capacity to think beyond their limitations. I believe Jabez's prayer was a request for God to help him think differently—outside of the proverbial box—so that he could live a blessed life. And that's exactly what God did.

This begs the question "How does God enlarge one's intellectual capacity?" The answer is through the transformational power of vision.

God doesn't give people powerful visions based on their education, pedigree, leadership style, or personality type. Visions are given to people who capture them and believe that what they perceive is possible. Ultimately it is God who puts a vision in your heart, just as He does His desires (Num. 12:6; Ps. 37:4).

God is always speaking, but are you capturing His thoughts? Are you disciplined enough to hear what He is conveying to you? Just as prayer, fasting, Bible study, and worship keep us attuned to God's voice, procuring a vision for your life is a spiritual discipline that keeps you in sync with God's will for your life.

Have you ever considered that your thoughts and ideas are spiritual entities—and that the spiritual realm is actually the causal realm? Let me clarify what I mean: When I speak of things that are spiritual, I am referring to that which is nonmaterial, incorporeal, intangible, conceptual, and transcendent. For example, virtues such as love, peace, respect, honor, and forgiveness are not visible to the natural eye but nevertheless exist and can be as healing as medicine or as freeing as a breath of fresh air. Likewise, a vision that you can see with your spiritual eyes can be as powerful as what you see with your natural eyes.

A vision is a divine mental preview of coming attractions. It's what you are able to see today as a potentiality for your tomorrow. Personally, I love going to the cinema. Believe it or not, what makes going to the movies exciting for me is not just the anticipation of the featured film but the coming attractions—the previews might even excite me more than the actual movie. I plan my moviegoing itinerary based on these trailers because they are not just exciting images of what *could* be but *will* be. They are not figments of someone's imagination but announcements of what I can expect to see at a future date. This allows me to anticipate and prepare for what I plan to see.

Just as movie previews pique your interest and stir up your zeal, a vision is God's appeal to you to stir up latent gifts, abilities, and talents so you can anticipate and prepare for the vision's actualization. Even as marketing experts craft scintillating images and catchphrases to grab your attention, God will rouse your senses and stimulate your spirit through illustrative details that vividly describe how He sees your future unfolding. Through the use of imagery and words that generate excitement and passion, your vision should be so dynamic that everyone who hears about it will be inspired to either get involved or pursue his or her own vision.

RISE TO MEET THE FUTURE

American inventor Charles Kettering was a man ahead of his time. He held more than 140 patents, and he invented or was instrumental in the development of refrigerator coolant, the electric self-starting ignition, quick-drying paint, an incubator for premature babies, the diesel locomotive engine, high-octane gasoline, and an aerial torpedo. In 1927 he founded the Kettering Foundation, which still publishes its widely read leadership journal, the *Kettering Review.* He graced the cover of *Time* magazine in 1933.

Kettering took an active interest in the future. He is commonly quoted as saying, "My interest is in the future because I am going to spend the rest of my life there."[1] He didn't wait for tomorrow to come to him; he reached out and grabbed it through vision.

Charles Kettering understood the value of ideas. He wasn't afraid of thinking beyond "the box," nor did he second-guess his capabilities. Whatever he needed to know he used his intellectual resources to procure. He was confident that with enough information and experience, he could solve any problem that presented itself—and at the turn of the twentieth century there were plenty of them to solve.

As we continue our march deeper into the twenty-first century, problems that need solving still abound. We can choose to wait for someone else to solve them, or approach them like Kettering did as rich opportunities to maximize our potential. He looked beyond the problem and saw what was possible. Do you just see the problem, or do you see what's possible? For many this question creates anxiety because they lack confidence in their ability to contribute to problem-solving efforts. But as Henry Ford, a contemporary of Kettering, is often quoted as saying, "Whether you believe you can do a thing or not, you are right."[2]

The world needs people who think they can, those who have a with-God-all-things-are-possible mind-set. Ask God to give you a possibility mind-set, an insatiable curiosity to discover what lies beyond the way things are or have always been, and the divine empowerment to find solutions, meet needs, and address issues. I want to encourage you today to step out in faith and become the kind of person who grabs hold of the future.

In examining Scripture, I have discovered you can actually prophesy greatness, success, and progress into your future. You can provoke your future and cause it to conform to God's original plan and purpose with vision and wisdom that comes from God (James 1:5). Look at what happened to an entire city when Elisha prophesied into its future.

> Then Elisha said, "Hear the word of the LORD. Thus says the LORD: 'Tomorrow about this time a seah of fine flour shall be sold for a shekel, and two seahs of barley for a shekel, at the gate of Samaria.'"
>
> So an officer on whose hand the king leaned answered the man of God and said, "Look, if the LORD would make windows in heaven, could this thing be?"
>
> And he said, "In fact, you shall see it with your eyes, but you shall not eat of it."…
>
> Then the people went out and plundered the tents of the Syrians. So a seah of fine flour was sold for a shekel, and two seahs of barley for a shekel, according to the word of the LORD. Now the king had appointed the officer on whose hand he leaned to have charge of the gate. But the people trampled him in the gate, and he died, just as the man of God had said, who spoke when the king came down to him. So it happened just as the man of God had

spoken to the king, saying, "Two seahs of barley for a shekel, and a seah of fine flour for a shekel, shall be sold tomorrow about this time in the gate of Samaria."

Then that officer had answered the man of God, and said, "Now look, if the LORD would make windows in heaven, could such a thing be?"

And he had said, "In fact, you shall see it with your eyes, but you shall not eat of it." And so it happened to him, for the people trampled him in the gate, and he died.

—2 KINGS 7:1–2, 16–20

I want to help you see with new eyes the unexplored opportunities on the horizon—the yet-to-be-charted seas and new social, cultural, spiritual, geopolitical, and industry-specific frontiers and breakthroughs that are waiting to be discovered. I want to challenge you to become a visionary for this generation—to see opportunities lying dormant in every problem and bring innovative ideas and solutions to the table with the potential to positively impact communities while changing the trajectory of humanity in the process.

HOW YOU SEE YOUR FUTURE BEGINS WITH HOW YOU SEE YOURSELF

The possibilities you are able to see depend on how you see yourself in the future. Let God help you see your life from His perspective (Jer. 29:11). How far you are able to see into your future depends on your willingness to discipline your mind and spirit through prayer and meditation on the Word of God. God will reveal how your potential will unfold according to His divine plans and purpose for your life. You will see your gifts and abilities finding expression on the grand stage of life and becoming synchronized with God's plan for humanity. Imagine the possibilities!

You will often hear me quote, "Your feet will never take you where your mind has never been." Those words have stuck with me for a long time now. They are why I want you to see yourself doing extraordinary things—creating, coaching, leading, writing, preaching, teaching, discovering, or building—as if they were reality. Let God paint His plans on the canvas of your mind. Spend time alone with Him and ask Him to show you the great things He has prepared for you to do and accomplish (1 Cor. 2:9–10). Let your faith, not your fears, motivate you. Trust God to empower you with wisdom to make your vision a reality. This principle is so essential to living a successful, victorious life that it has been the backbone of much of what I teach. It is the foundational principle of this book, along with the Scripture verse much akin to it: "Where there is no vision, the people perish" (Prov. 29:18, KJV).

Vision is simply a matter of how you see yourself in the future. It is acquiring a fresh perspective for your life from God's vantage point. Just like when you go to the movies, a vision is a divine announcement of "coming attractions."

---

*Your feet will never take you where
your mind has never been.*

How you see the future is contingent upon what you believe is possible for you and your family, community, and nation; it is contingent upon what you believe about your potential for making something happen. What do you believe about your potential to live the life you've imagined? I want to encourage you that God

9

does not play games with our minds. He will never give you a desire to do something and not empower you to do it. "Delight yourself also in the LORD, and He shall give you the desires of your heart. Commit your way to the LORD, trust also in Him, and He shall bring it to pass" (Ps. 37:4–5). He will never give you a vision and not provide the resources to make it a reality. "If you can believe, all things are possible" (Mark 9:23).

Vision is not something you conjure up in your own imagination, but through prayerful consideration you discern the will of God for your life (Job 32:8). Your vision should line up with the Word of God and be a way you can fulfill your part of the Great Commission: "Go therefore and make disciples of all nations, baptizing them in the name of the Father and of the Son and of the Holy Spirit, teaching them to observe all things I have commanded you" (Matt. 28:19–20, MEV). Once you have your vision, you can then discipline yourself to write the vision down and put feet to what you have written.

YOUR FOCUS DETERMINES YOUR FUTURE

What is the lens through which you look at challenges and possibilities? Do you see them as something other people are more innately wired to overcome or take advantage of? Are you more focused on potential limitations or potential successes, the possible risks or promising rewards?

Your focus is subject to your mind-set and paradigm of success— how you set your mind frames your mental model. What you believe to be true about a situation, your country, and this world is what you'll likely experience. And what you believe about your circumstances is largely determined by what you believe to be true about yourself. Your belief system colors your expectations with the brilliance of its hue and informs you of what you are worthy of receiving, achieving, earning, learning, and being. "Your chances of success in any undertaking," writes author Robert Collier, "can always be measured by your belief in yourself."[3]

Vision gives you the ability to see with new and untainted eyes. Perhaps the greatest—or at least most renowned—artist, architect, and engineer to have ever lived, Leonardo da Vinci, attributed his success to knowing how to see. *Sapere vedere*, Latin for "knowing how to see," was his personal motto. He developed well the art of seeing before he painted masterpieces such as *The Last Supper* or the *Mona Lisa*—or conceiving innovations such as the helicopter, parachute, and scuba gear.

Da Vinci was a man of vision. He was the quintessential visionary, and he was a key figure during the Renaissance, along with others including Michelangelo di Lodovico Buonarroti Simoni. What set them apart was their ability to see differently: to see David or the Madonna hidden in a block of stone, to look at the sky and design ways to reach it, or to view a blank ceiling and envision the Sistine Chapel. Their ability to see beyond the confines of stone or even gravity transcended natural reason—it could almost be considered a supernatural sight.

The word *vision* is from the Old French *vision,* meaning "presence, sight; view, look, appearance; dream, supernatural sight." The French word is from the Latin *visionem*, meaning "act of seeing, sight, thing seen." In the time of Leonardo da Vinci and Michelangelo it was a word used to describe "something seen in the imagination or in the supernatural."[4] I think of it as someone shining a light into a dark room, exposing everything that the room contains.

Sometimes that darkness can be what blinds us to our own personal potential. Sometimes we must simply speak into that darkness and declare, "Let there be light!" We need to tap into Christ within us. He is the light of our souls (John 1:4), we are created in His image (Gen. 1:27), and through Him we are becoming more and more like Him: the light of the world (2 Cor. 3:18; John 8:12).

> It started when God said, "Light up the darkness!" and our lives filled up with light.
> —2 CORINTHIANS 4:6, THE MESSAGE

Those of us who believe Jesus Christ is indeed the life and light of men should be taking the lead in illuminating the yet unseen solutions needed in an increasingly dark world. In this age you and I are called to be the light that shines through the darkness (Isa. 60:2; Matt. 5:14). Knowing who you are and who you're called to become in Christ is the first step in learning how to see yourself and what you're truly capable of. Jesus promised, "If you follow me, you won't be stumbling through the darkness, for living light will flood your path" (John 8:12, TLB).

The light you've been given by God is supernatural insight into future possibilities. When I think of the word *insight*, I think of the night-vision goggles and binoculars issued to soldiers that allow them to see in the dark. Likewise, you have been equipped as a soldier of heaven (2 Tim. 2:3–4) with supernatural night vision! It was God who said, "Let light shine out of darkness" and thereby "made his light shine in our hearts to give us the light of the knowledge" (2 Cor. 4:6, NIV). We should be able to see where others cannot. We should be seeing the beautiful form hidden in what seems like impenetrable rock, or gravity-defying structures that have yet to take flight. We should be speaking life and light into what seem to be dead and dark places.

THE FAR AND DISTANT SHORE

As you begin to set sail toward the tomorrows of your future, you must know what type of vessel you are (Rom. 9:21). For it is with this revelation that you can pierce into the darkness of your potential to see the amazing treasure that lies beneath (2 Cor. 4:7). The Bible tells us that "the fear of the LORD is the beginning of wisdom" (Ps. 111:10; Prov. 9:10). But there is also wisdom in knowing and understanding yourself. The ancient Greek aphorism "Know thyself" was the basis for Socrates' statement that "the unexamined life is not worth living." Socrates' student Plato taught that the essence of knowledge is self-knowledge.

Knowing who you are, why you are here, what you value, what you believe, and what you stand for is not only powerfully informative but also empowering. Becoming grounded in the knowledge of who you are as a unique individual is how you mature spiritually. You must be intimately acquainted with your gifts and callings to become an effective and fully functioning member of the body of Christ (Rom. 12:3–8). Being true to yourself—living and speaking your truth based on God's truth—is an act of integrity. As Polonius said in Shakespeare's *Hamlet*, "This above all: to thine own self be true; and it must follow, as the night the day, thou canst not then be false to any man."[5]

Become the Christopher Columbus of your own destiny. If you are to reach that far and distant shore of your dream-inspired destiny, you must first and foremost become a *seaworthy vessel*. And in order to become seaworthy, you must know what kind of vessel God created you to be—whether a clipper, a frigate, a galleon, a schooner, or a yacht. Knowing what kind of vessel God crafted you to be will enable you to better navigate the seas ahead. There are a number of tools you can use to gain greater self-understanding.

Behavioral profiles such as DiSC can be extraordinarily helpful in broadening your self-knowledge, as can the Barrett Personal Values Assessment.

Although you most likely have a general sense of your greatest strengths and weaknesses, and perhaps even some potential opportunities and threats, I encourage you to take a closer look at what you may not have been aware of before. Take a look under the hull—your mind! Have you ever seen a boat on the shore lifted up off the ground on large cinder blocks? There are times when it is beneficial to put yourself in dry dock, so to speak. Take time to prayerfully examine the amazing things God is attempting to reveal to you about your future. Examine your faith. Like Abraham, are you "fully convinced that what [God] had promised He [is] also able to perform" (Rom. 4:21)? Do you really believe that God is able to provide the resources to achieve every vision He has given you? Only by taking a candid look at what's going on beneath the surface of your spiritual life can you clear away the barnacles of unbelief, doubt, and other negative emotions that attach themselves to the underside of your soul. Then you'll go farther and faster, free of what may have been unseen negative entanglements.[6]

When we talk about the transformational power of vision, we are largely talking about a state of mind: "the ability to think about or plan the future with imagination."[7] In the chapters ahead we will explore how to effectively harness the power of imagination. Your imagination and thoughts are vital to effectively steering you toward the fulfillment of your dreams. If you've ever heard me speak, you've heard me say, "You are always one decision away from living the life of your dreams." Your life today is the sum total of every decision you've made. You must choose to go after the vision God has given you. You must choose to do what He has called you to do in order to be who He has called you to be. You must choose to focus on the future He promised you. Every thought you choose to entertain affects the course of your destiny. "You create your future by envisioning it," said Jack Canfield.[8] Can you imagine how great your future will be once your life is in sync with God's plan?

You have a race to run and a bright future ahead of you (Heb. 12:1; Rev. 21). You've been given everything you need to accomplish whatever God has called you to do (2 Pet. 1:3). You have the mind of Christ (1 Cor. 2:16); the favor of God (Prov. 8:35); spiritual gifts, talents, and abilities (1 Cor. 12:4–11); and the wisdom of heaven just for the asking (James 1:5). What will you do with what you've been given?

PIONEER A NEW FRONTIER

A new world awaits those willing to discover it. I have always been inspired by the words of University of Kansas Chancellor E. H. Lindley, who in the early twentieth century encouraged students to "develop the spirit of the old pioneers who were not afraid of new problems,"[9] and James E. Faust, who admonished his listeners to "become pioneers of the future with all its exciting opportunities."[10]

This takes faith, and faith can be risky business. The world was built by people who were not afraid to take risks. They were the pioneers who were not afraid of the wilderness, the scientists who were not afraid of being ridiculed, the thought leaders who were not afraid of progress, the politicians who were not afraid to challenge the status quo, the theologians who were not afraid of being called a heretic, the slaves who were not afraid of dying, the youth who were not afraid of asking "Why?" or "Why not?" and the dreamers who were not afraid to take action.

If you are going to leave the shores of the familiar in order to navigate great oceans of success (Ps. 107:23–24), it will take some degree of risk. If you are going to realize your dreams and do something great, pursue a degree, become a best-selling author, build a children's home in a third-world country, start a church, open a crisis pregnancy center, or establish a foundation dedicated to educating underprivileged children, you must accept the fact that a degree of risk is involved. "What if I fail?" you might ask. "What if you succeed?" is my response!

This is the difference between those who take risks and those who play it safe: those who play it safe operate from sight, and those who take risks operate from vision. In his celebrated speech "The Strenuous Life," Theodore Roosevelt famously stated,

> Far better is it to dare mighty things, to win glorious triumphs, even though checkered by failure, than to take rank with those poor spirits who neither enjoy much nor suffer much, because they live in the gray twilight that knows not victory nor defeat.[11]

Many people have an "I want to" in their spirit, but they allow fear to immobilize them until it dissolves into "I can't" or "I'm afraid." Dare to change the "I want to" into "I must," and "I can't" into "with the help of God, I will." (See 2 Timothy 1:7.) This kind of attitude takes courage. It means that you have to move beyond the self-imposed limitations and excuses. General Matthew B. Ridgway said:

> There are two kinds of courage, physical and moral, and he who would be a true leader must have both. Both are the products of the character-forming process, of

the development of self-control, self-discipline, physical endurance, of knowledge of one's job and, therefore, of confidence. These qualities minimize fear and maximize sound judgment under pressure and—with some of that indispensable stuff called luck—often bring success from seemingly hopeless situations.[12]

If you were to critically analyze everything you do on a daily basis, from driving your car, to flying on an airplane, to walking your dog, each involves some degree of risk. By changing your thoughts about doing what you really want regardless of the perceived risk, you set a powerful intention in motion. You rise to the challenge of breaking free from limiting beliefs and habit patterns that keep you stuck. By choosing to change your belief about your right to progress and prosper, you give yourself permission to succeed. By getting rid of self-destructive habits that undermine your potential, you are able to acquire new habits that foster new behaviors, attitudes, and beliefs. By creating a no-excuse zone in your mind, you will arouse the courage to pursue the life of your dreams.

Robert Schuller, one of America's twenty-first-century luminary pastors, asked, "What goals would you be setting for yourself if you knew you could not fail?"[13] Most people waste their time focusing on the potential for failure. However, even though failure is possible, keep in mind that failure is simply the tuition you pay for future success. A similar question you might ask yourself is "What would I do if I only had a few months left to live?"

These questions should stimulate your faith and inspire you to leap into your future. Taking those leaps is the starting point of personal greatness. John Mason said:

If you never take risks, you'll never accomplish great things. Everybody dies, but not everyone has lived.[14]

Potential is all you can be but have not yet become, all you can do but have not yet done, how far you can reach but have not yet tried. Vision is the catalyst that ignites your potential.

Dare to look within to see your true potential, and then shift your focus from what lies within to the possibilities that are directly in front of you, then to what lies months and years down the road. May every lid and limitation be blown off your life. Don't limit yourself to what you think is possible. Push past your current limitations and reach higher. People commonly overestimate what they can do in one year but underestimate what they can do in five. Don't sell yourself short. Take the long view. Head for the far and distant shore by pioneering your own new frontier.

> Man is the master of thought, the moulder of character, and the maker and shaper of condition, environment, and destiny. As a being of Power, Intelligence, and Love...man holds the key to every situation, and contains within himself that transforming and regenerative agency by which he may make himself what he wills.
>
> —JAMES ALLEN

> You control your future, your destiny. What you think about comes about. By recording your dreams and goals on paper, you set in motion the process of becoming the person you most want to be. Put your future in good hands—your own.
>
> —MARK VICTOR HANSEN

· · ·

CHAPTER TWO

Leave Ordinary Behind

But one thing I do, forgetting those things which
are behind and reaching forward to those things
which are ahead, I press toward the goal for the
prize of the upward call of God in Christ Jesus.
—PHILIPPIANS 3:13–14

Sometimes all it takes is a subtle shift in
perspective, an opening of the mind, an
intentional pause and reset, or a new route to
start to see new options and new possibilities.
—KRISTIN ARMSTRONG

THE JOURNEY OF a thousand miles does not only begin with the first step; it begins with the first step of faith. Faith takes you into the uncharted waters of greatness (Ps. 107:24). The journey of life requires navigating these waters. If you think that greatness is not for you, think again. You serve a great God who has great plans for your life. Whatever you are currently thinking about doing, being, or acquiring, think bigger! Refuse to settle for a "this-is-good-enough" mentality, because once you do, you will live an average, mediocre life—a life that lacks luster.

I'm here to tell you that mediocrity is not in your genes (2 Pet. 1:4). You have greatness in your DNA! First John 4:4 (KJV) states, "Ye are of God...greater is he that is in you, than he that is in the world." The operative words here are *of God*, meaning you come from God. You were born to be great! You are wired for greatness! The opposite of greatness is not just smallness and insignificance but also averageness and mediocrity. When you settle for living a life of mediocrity, it is because you either refuse to believe in your greatness, you don't think you deserve better, or you've refused to challenge yourself to reach beyond the threshold of what is comfortable and familiar. It is about failing to choose the best of what God has for you—but instead choosing to live among the clutter of the common, not wanting to stick out for fear of being misjudged, misunderstood, or rejected.

It is a shame that some people have mistaken being average for being humble—as God's best will for humanity. But this is a tragic deception. A mind-set that gives way to mediocrity fails to recognize that God created human beings in His image as representatives of His excellence and glory (Isa. 43:7). Most people don't embrace the fullness of their potential for fear of being considered arrogant. Often people are called arrogant when they refuse to bow to low expectations or have a grand vision for improving themselves and the world around them. To reiterate, you serve a great God who created you for so much more when He created you in His image and after His likeness. Therefore greatness runs in your genes! Greatness is not about being better than someone else but being the best version of yourself.

When you put your greatness on display, you glorify God as

the *light* and *salt* in the earth (Matt. 5:13–16). To have an average mentality is to resign yourself to a life of unreached and unfulfilled potential, cheating the world of the things that God has placed in you for the good of humanity. You aren't an underachiever— you are an overcomer (Rev. 12:11). Even if you already see your-self as a success, you are always capable of reaching higher and achieving more in Christ. Your potential in the kingdom is limit-less. Whatever you focus on and truly desire, be it a vision, dream, or goal, with God's help you can achieve (Phil. 4:13). Get rid of your average mind-set. An average mind-set is destructive because it will never challenge you to expand your horizon, think outside of the box, or break out of a don't-rock-the-boat state of mind. The status quo is popular because it requires no discipline, nor does it require you to grow spiritually as you progress and prosper.

Greatness is not about being better than someone else but being the best version of yourself.

Vision brings you into a higher spiritual plane of growth and development. Spiritual growth will lead you into realms above and beyond what your natural mind can imagine. Vision calls you higher. Your ascension into higher realms of power, influence, and affluence requires you to pull away from vision assassins who don't believe in your greatness. It requires you to operate in the realm of courage where you embrace everything God wants you to be. (See Joshua 1:6–9.) If life were a game, it would require you to get off the sidelines and onto center court. It would require you to grab the ball and run with it. So get some skin in the game. Get rid of your wishful thinking. Put feet to your dreams. Weigh anchor and set sail. Your future is filled with unlimited opportunities, so go for it!

LIFE WILL GIVE YOU WHAT YOU DESIRE

In the story of Lot there is a verse where angels are urging Lot to leave Sodom and Gomorrah. From this I've learned that life will give you what you desire:

> The angel said to him, "See, I am doing what you ask. I will not destroy this town that you have spoken about. Hurry and run there. For I cannot do anything until you get there." So the name given to the town was Zoar.
>
> —GENESIS 19:21–22, NLV

The translation of the word Zoar literally means insignificance or smallness.[1] Why would anyone want to live in Zoar when God had something greater for him? (See John 14:2–3.) Why would anyone ask to move in the direction of insignificance when God promises to fulfill the desires of his heart (Ps. 37:4)—let alone do above and beyond what he can dream or imagine (Eph. 3:20)?

So many people think they have no options in life. They have been trained to think small. But this is a state that we accept as a result of what I call a "satanic seduction" that has people walking around in a spiritual stupor, unaware of the magnificent life Jesus offers us all.

> The thief cometh not, but for to steal, and to kill, and to destroy: I am come that they might have life, and that they might have it more abundantly.
>
> —JOHN 10:10, KJV

Living with lack is not the desire of God for your life. It is what the enemy of your soul desires—he desires for you to be deceived into believing you have to accept leftovers and handouts. But that's not the case. You were born for bigness, not for begging—for prosperity, not poverty. When you believe this and receive this, eventually you will become this. So believe it! Receive it! Dare to become it!

God never intended for you to accept smallness and insignificance as a way of life. He did not create you to live with small thinking. He wants you to think big, expect big things, desire big things, and live large in the largeness of Himself. This is why vision is so important. It helps you get rid of your small-mindedness. You should want more for yourself, for your family, for your business, for your neighborhood, and for your country. What do you really want for yourself and your loved ones? Not only does God give you the desire to desire, but He puts *His* desires in your heart. The desires you have were first authored—and then given to you—by Him (Ps. 37:4).

To desire anything less than what God desires for you is a travesty. God will never disappoint you. You can trust Him to come through for you (Prov. 13:12; Heb. 11:6). Hear God's promise:

> Therefore I say to you, whatever things you ask when you pray, believe that you receive them, and you will have them.
> —MARK 11:24

"GRITITUDE"

Leaving ordinary behind for a life of greatness takes perseverance and mental strength. It takes an attitude of grit—what I call "grititude." You are only as strong as your faith, courage, convictions, and determination to make the next move and take the next step in spite of the bumps, turns, and collisions. No matter how challenging the situation, how dark the days, or how dismal the hours, you can always make life better the moment you recognize that God is at work in the wreckage. It doesn't matter whether you fly, run, walk, creep, or crawl as long as you keep inching forward. You will eventually collide with your best days waiting just beyond the zone of discomfort and disappointment.

The call of Abraham was a call to greatness, but it required him to leave the familiarity of his environment, his relational constellation, and his source of resources.

> Now the LORD had said to Abram: "Get out of your country, from your family and from your father's house, to a land that I will show you. I will make you a great nation; I will bless you and make your name great; and you shall be a blessing. I will bless those who bless you, and I will curse him who curses you; and in you all the families of the earth shall be blessed."
>
> —GENESIS 12:1–4

God told Abraham to leave the familiar and pioneer something new. We have new frontiers before us waiting to be discovered. There is a sea of opportunities in every field, industry, system, and discipline that stretches out ahead of us. God is bidding us to walk into new realms of faith and experience dominion as He originally planned. To quote Napoleon Hill, "Never has there been a time more favorable to pioneers than the present."[2]

It's easy to look at the negative: sin, poverty, corruption, despotic governments, gang violence, human trafficking, drug trafficking, political unrest, terrorism, global warming, global recession, unemployment, underemployment, and the like. We live in what the military has dubbed a VUCA environment—a world characterized by volatility, uncertainty, complexity, and ambiguity. But in the midst of uncertainty, we need to remember that we serve a God "with whom there is no variation or shadow of turning" (James 1:17).

While most people are disconcerted and find themselves overwhelmed with the task of managing the present, we, the people of God and citizens of the kingdom, can look beyond the circumstances of these tumultuous times and by faith see the sun rising just beyond the horizon. While others see obstacles, by faith we see opportunity appearing with the dawning of a new day.

There's a somewhat obscure revelation found in a familiar scripture of the Bible that I've used to motivate myself in the pursuit of fulfilling my purpose.

> When the Son of Man returns, it will be like it was in Noah's day. In those days before the flood, the people were enjoying banquets and parties and weddings right up to the time Noah entered his boat. People didn't realize what was going to happen until the flood came and swept them all away. That is the way it will be when the Son of Man comes.
>
> —MATTHEW 24:37–39, NLT

This scripture helped me understand that while those were Noah's days, these are yours and mine. Just like Noah, you don't have to be swept away by the currents of cultural change. You can be like Noah, fulfilling your assignment, maximizing your potential, and moving humanity forward according to God's revealed plan for your life.

As morbid as this statement may seem, someday your life will come to an end. There will be no more someday-soon days, I'll-do-it-tomorrow days, when-I-finish-my-degree days, or when-the-children-grow-up days. There will be no more sleeping-through-a-beautiful-sunrise days, I-should-have-done-it days, I-forgot-to-do-it days, or I-don't-feel-like-doing-it days. There will be no more hours, minutes, or seconds. It will not matter what you acquired, remembered, or forgot. Your fears, doubts, apprehensions, frustrations, and disappointments will finally disappear. So too will your opportunities to live deliberately and intentionally. The Bible says that there is "a time for every purpose under heaven" (Eccles. 3:1), and the time to fulfill your purpose is now. Vision, therefore, becomes important because it keeps you focused on the main thing—your purpose and your assignment. Vision gives you the nudge you need to discipline your mind when you are tempted to put things off—to pay attention to your dreams and get on with bringing them to pass.

Don't keep putting off your dreams and placing your goals on the back burner. Find your place in the unfolding of God's plan for humanity.[3] Finding that place can seem like a daunting task, but when you examine the life of history makers, you will see this thread of truth: God used them during humanity's most critical times and greatest moments of pain, and then paired that pain with their greatest passion. And when pain is paired with passion, purpose becomes crystal clear.

THERE IS BETTER THAN *HERE*

Your vision will take you on your unique path. That path may lead you beyond the status quo and the conventions of culture that define the realities of life within your community or country.

Vision is the ultimate adventure that will help you discover the person you were always meant to be, and you will also discover your true worth in the process.

Frederick Douglass, philosopher, activist, and author, found the courage to risk running away from his master's plantation to pursue his vision of literacy and freedom. He challenged himself to learn how to read, and he eventually went on to live a remarkable life because he refused to give in to the status quo of slavery and ignorance.

> My free life began on the third of September, 1838. On the morning of the fourth of that month, after an anxious and most perilous but safe journey, I found myself in the big city of New York, a FREE MAN—one more added to the mighty throng which, like the confused waves of the troubled sea, surged to and fro between the lofty walls of Broadway.... But my gladness was short-lived, for I was not yet out of the reach and power of the slave-holders.[4]

Faith often has an element of risk. Pursuing your vision will at times take you on risky excursions as you navigate the currents of change, the headwinds of failure, and the riptides of emotional turmoil or uncertainty. All risk is not created equal. But staying where you are can ultimately be more risky than reaching for your dreams. You risk your entire future for a false sense of safety, comfort, and security. When the tension builds up inside of you to explore doing something more, it's usually God tapping you on the shoulder to let you know it's time to move on.

Moving on means that you must risk your comfort and convenience, even your support and understanding, in order to pursue your passion, realize your vision, and fulfill your dreams. It is a sink or swim, perish or survive kind of mentality that says, "I am prepared to risk everything to accomplish that thing I was born to do." What you are willing to risk is based on what you want and what you value. Ben Carson once said, "It's very important for people to know themselves and understand what their value system is, because if you don't know what your value system is, then you don't know what risks are worth taking and which ones are worth avoiding."[5]

For Frederick Douglass, what he valued was freedom and an education. He was willing to risk everything, even his life, to obtain it. Douglass weighed the pros and cons of action and attitude, of responsibilities and opportunities, of his vision of freedom contrasted with the conditions that made up his reality—and freedom won out. For him, freedom was better than slavery, and education was better than ignorance. Douglass risked much, but he achieved success. He became well-known as an orator and author, and toward the end of his life he served his country as consul general to Haiti and chargé d'affaires for Santo Domingo.

John F. Kennedy said, "There are risks and costs to a program of action. But they are far less than the long-range risks and costs of comfortable inaction."[6] Success and progress come from taking calculated risks. The beautiful thing about taking calculated risks is that you will either achieve your goals or learn something new in the process. Either way you win, even if success is derived from the acquisition of additional knowledge and the accumulation of experience.

The Greek historian Herodotus wrote, "Great successes are not won except by great risks."[7] In other words, think about it only long enough to determine whether it is worth the effort—whether you or the world will be better for it. If so, don't hesitate—take the risk. Risk is inextricably connected to success. Those who are unwilling to take risks are bound not to succeed; at the same time, in taking risks, one must also accept full responsibility for the outcomes—both the successes and the failures.

Jesus said, "Risk your life and get more than you ever dreamed of. Play it safe and end up holding the bag" (Luke 19:26, THE MESSAGE). When you leave the ordinary en route to the extraordinary, don't use the rearview mirror in an attempt to find your way. Forget those things which are behind, reach forward to the things up ahead, and press toward the goal of the high calling of God (Phil. 3:13–14). Take a calculated risk, and by faith dare to inhale the sweet fragrance of success.

EXERCISE UNCOMPROMISING FAITH

Abraham lived in a time when serving God was not popular. God gave him two options: choose to listen to the culture, or choose to listen to Him. In a world filled with morally and spiritually dissenting voices, you have to have the courage to choose to listen to God. Abraham chose to listen to God, to believe in the unlimited possibilities that lay ahead of him, and to trust God in the process. He did "as the LORD had spoken to him" (Gen. 12:4).

In his classic book *The Path of Least Resistance*, Robert Fritz writes, "If you limit your choices only to what seems possible or reasonable…you disconnect yourself from what you truly want, and all you have left is a compromise."[8] Don't compromise your vision for doing great things because of the challenges inherent in our times. The moment you compromise in one area, it can lead to compromise in all areas. Accepting the status quo is resigning yourself to being a product of your environment, a victim of circumstances, or a combination of both. Don't compromise your future because the present is challenging. Compromise leads to catastrophe. You have a bright future ahead of you. Don't be like the masses who have lost their hope because they feel there is nothing they can do to escape their current circumstances. You don't have to live among those that have lost hope (Eph. 2:12–13).

Hebrews 6:12 instructs us to find someone we can emulate. To be more specific, it states that we should "imitate those who through faith and patience inherit what has been promised" (NIV). Abraham is recognized in Hebrews 11 as a man of faith: "By faith Abraham obeyed when he was called to go out to the place which he would receive as an inheritance. And he went out, not knowing where he was going" (v. 8). But Hebrews 11 also talks about others who stretched their faith toward both the revealed plan of God and the God of the revealed plan. God has promised a better end for your life than how it began. (See Ecclesiastes 7:8.) It will take faith to navigate the journey from the known to the unknown. We must "walk by faith, not by sight" (2 Cor. 5:7). Why is faith so important? As we journey through life, we are bombarded by storms—and it is faith that empowers you to overcome them all.

> For whatever is born of God overcomes the world. And this is the victory that has overcome the world—our faith. Who is he who overcomes the world, but he who believes that Jesus is the Son of God?
>
> —1 JOHN 5:4–5

Just as I have, you fight so many battles in life, but in the midst of spiritual warfare it is your faith that protects you, your vision, your dreams, and your goals. Paul gave us clear instructions in his letter to the Ephesians: "Above all, taking the shield of faith with which you will be able to quench all the fiery darts of the wicked one" (Eph. 6:16).

LEARN TO SEE WITH NEW EYES

Faith also helps you to see with new eyes. God told Abraham to look out past where he stood into the distance, "northward, southward, eastward, and westward" (Gen. 13:14). Why? Because only what he was able to see would He be able to give him: "for all the land which you see I give to you and your descendants forever....Arise, walk in the land through its length and its width, for I give it to you" (Gen. 13:15–17).

I believe that this generation is suffering from spiritual blindness. Because of a lack of faith we are not able to see the things that God wants to bring into our lives (Heb. 11:1). Things God has prepared for you before the foundation of the world are not always apparent to the natural eye and thus require you to tap into the realm of faith to acquire them (Deut. 29:29).

There are things that are invisible to the naked eye. Take, for example, hydrogen and oxygen; we cannot see them, but when they combine through a chemical reaction, they become a visible substance called water. The same thing happens when sodium and chlorine come together to form table salt. These molecules can actually exist side by side without ever being transformed into a visible substance. But when the molecules react with each other, they are transformed into substances we can both see and use. Similarly faith is an invisible process that allows us to respond continuously to God's Word, producing visible effects in our lives. These things are revealed to us by the Spirit of God.

But as it is written: "Eye has not seen, nor ear heard, nor have entered into the heart of man the things which God has prepared for those who love Him." But God has revealed them to us through His Spirit. For the Spirit searches all things, yes, the deep things of God. For what man knows the things of a man except the spirit of the man which is in him? Even so no one knows the things of God except the Spirit of God. Now we have received, not the spirit of the world, but the Spirit who is from God, that we might know the things that have been freely given to us by God.

—1 Corinthians 2:9–12

God is a God of revelation. The word *revelation* comes from the Greek word *apokalupto*, meaning "to uncover, lay open what has been veiled or covered up; disclose, make bare; to make known, make manifest, disclose what before was unknown."[9] In 2 Kings we read the account of Elisha's servant who at first was unable to see the armies of God surrounding their enemies. Then he had a revelation. Elisha prayed that God would open his servant's eyes, and God did:

And when the servant of the man of God arose early and went out, there was an army, surrounding the city with horses and chariots. And his servant said to him, "Alas, my master! What shall we do?"

So he answered, "Do not fear, for those who are with us are more than those who are with them." And Elisha prayed, and said, "Lord, I pray, open his eyes that he may see." Then the Lord opened the eyes of the young man, and he saw. And behold, the mountain was full of horses and chariots of fire all around Elisha.

—2 KINGS 6:15–17

"And behold, the mountain was full of horses and chariots of fire..." From this text we learn that faith sees what the average person is blind to. To leave behind the ordinary, you must learn to see the extraordinary. Your life will move in the direction of what you are able to see by faith. See bigger, broader, farther, higher. Practice seeing more expansively. Exercise your faith to grab hold of the kind of revelation that will open your eyes to the kingdom at work in your life. A revelation is simply a "revealing" of what more is possible in Christ.

...that the God of our Lord Jesus Christ, the Father of glory, may give to you the spirit of wisdom and revelation in the knowledge of Him, the eyes of your understanding being enlightened; that you may know what is the hope of His calling, what are the riches of the glory of His inheritance in the saints, and what is the exceeding greatness of His power toward us who believe, according to the working of His mighty power.

—EPHESIANS 1:17–19

BE WILLING TO GO WHERE YOU'VE NEVER BEEN

T. S. Eliot said, "Only those who will risk going too far can possibly find out how far one can go."[10] You cannot live an extraordinary life by remaining ordinary. It takes faith, courage, and grit to break cultural molds, national mores, social and political limitations, and family expectations.

Reach for the stars! Shoot for the moon! Elevate your life by daring to go higher. (See Colossians 3:1–3.) Living in the realm of possibility is where great achievers inhale the sweet air of success. Most people never break free from the status quo because they are unwilling to risk going out on a limb. But the end of the branch is where the sweetest fruit lies.

Learn to become the kind of visionary that raises the bar and levels up the people around you. Dare to join the ranks of those who push humanity forward.

> All things are possible to him who believes.
>
> —MARK 9:23

> Ask, and it will be given to you; seek, and you will find; knock, and it will be opened to you. For everyone who asks receives, and he who seeks finds, and to him who knocks it will be opened.
>
> —MATTHEW 7:7–8

• • •

CHAPTER THREE

Set Your Course Toward Tomorrow

There is nothing like [a] dream to create the future.
—VICTOR HUGO

Let us make our future now, and let us
make our dreams tomorrow's reality.
—MALALA YOUSAFZAI

HISTORY HAS BEEN marred by wars, rioting, despotic leadership, geopolitical challenges, ethnic cleansing, environmental erosion, and diseases that threatened to wipe out all of humanity. Yet in spite of these threats to our very existence, we are able to look through the pages of history books to identify individuals who kept hope alive and pointed us to the possibility of a better and brighter future by the power of their vision.

Proverbs tells us that "where there is no vision, the people perish" (Prov. 29:18, KJV)—they stumble in the darkness of despair. Lacking hope, they lose their way and eventually fail to thrive. But those visionaries who changed the course of history would not let that happen. Their bold ideas provoked us to change and inspired us to believe that we could overcome the challenges of the day—and we did.

It was the vision of ordinary individuals willing to risk failure and sometimes even death that has been key in the fight against colonialism, apartheid, authoritarianism, preventable disease, segregation, poverty, and illiteracy, to name a few. These visionaries hailed from every corner of the earth. They came from a diversity of backgrounds, ethnicities, and religious persuasions. They were doctors and ditch diggers, emancipators and engineers, common folk and rich folk, freemen and slaves, politicians and poets, environmentalists and economists, scientists and theologians.

Visionaries such as Martin Luther King Jr., Winston Churchill, Mahatma Gandhi, Nelson Mandela, Sojourner Truth, John F. Kennedy, Jane Goodall, Andrew Carnegie, Henry Ford, William Booth, D. L. Moody, Aimee Semple-McPherson, Oral Roberts, Billy Graham, Desmond Tutu, Billy Sunday, Rachel Carson, Vandana Shiva, Steven Jobs, and Walt Disney, along with a myriad of others, helped foster peace, technological advance, medical breakthroughs, and new economies, as well as new moral and ethical ways of thinking and living. I am impressed by the biographies of these visionaries that I have read over the years and inspired by their stories. But the greatest visionary ever to live, in my opinion, was Jesus Christ. He had a vision to save all of humanity and restore us back to our original state as heaven's representatives.

Vision is perhaps one of the most important spiritual forces in the world. By it lives are enhanced, purpose is actualized, and potential is maximized. It is a force that has shaped our world and fostered the progress of humanity. It is an essential factor for technological advancement, medical and scientific breakthroughs, community development, economic growth, and other accomplishments. It is a key element that helps shape our collective and individual lives.

Vision requires the use of the mind—and we all have one! Your mind is an idea-generating and innovative machine. It has no lids or limitations, except those that have been self-imposed. Your mind is powerful and can propel you to do so many extraordinary things—*once you understand how to harness its power* (2 Cor. 10:4–5). One idea is all it takes to create a beautiful work of art. One spark of inspiration is all it takes to compose a symphony. One vision for something better is all it takes to change the trajectory of a nation. In the words of Antoine de Saint-Exupéry, "A rock pile ceases to be a rock pile the moment a single man contemplates it, bearing within him the image of a cathedral."[1] What extraordinary possibility are you able to see when you look at your ordinary circumstances?

However, vision is not only the art of imagining; it is also the ability to bring what you've imagined to pass. Imagine what you could do if you did more than just think about doing something. Don't just imagine the possibilities—take action now to realize the life you've imagined living, the things you've imagined doing, the industries you've imagined impacting, the people you've imagined influencing, and the world you've imagined changing for the better. Begin to turn your rock pile into a cathedral, even if only one stone at a time. With the map of your vision before you, set your course to sail toward a better tomorrow.

SETTING THE RIGHT COURSE

New York Times best-selling author Richard Paul Evans recently came out with a new book titled *The Broken Road*. It's about a man who mid-career, despite great material success, wonders if he has wasted his life pursuing the wrong goals. It's a story of second chances. It reminds me of the redemption of the fictitious Ebenezer Scrooge in *A Christmas Carol*. That Christmas what a beautiful day dawns when he realizes there is still time to redirect his life. It's a terrible thing to live with regret but an even worse thing to die with it. This does not have to be you. You have an opportunity to live your life with purpose and to accomplish some great things within your lifetime.

The author of *The 7 Habits of Highly Effective People*, Stephen R. Covey, warns against working "harder and harder at climbing the ladder of success only to discover it's leaning against the wrong wall."[2] Too many people come to the end of their lives with misgivings or disappointment—or to the end of the road, so to speak, only to find they've been on the wrong road all along. These people failed to begin with the end in mind. They neglected to look ahead and identify where they hoped to go, let alone design a map to get there.

We must deliberately pursue a deeply meaningful vision, become clear on the nature of our truest desires, and intentionally set a course to fulfill them. Spend quality time with God. Allow Him to fill your heart, mind, and soul with vision. Without a vision, wrote King Solomon, people go astray (Prov. 29:18). Other translations make clear that the kind of vision that will take you where you truly want to go is guided by God; it is divinely inspired. (See Proverbs 29:18, NLT, NLV, NCV, TLB.) When your vision is infused with God's purposes for your life, it will keep you on the right course—just like bumpers keep a bowling ball headed toward the pins. It's when people ignore that inner voice calling them in a certain direction that they veer off course!

Visions are course correctors. I have heard of senior executives changing their career paths because of a compelling vision when they "should" have been thinking about retiring. I've heard of carpenters who became doctors and doctors who became carpenters because of a vision. I've heard of psychologists who became teachers, pharmacists who became farmers, social workers who became art directors, scientists who became massage therapists, ex-convicts who became judges, and soldiers who became ballroom dancers, all because of a vision.

THE LAND OF TOMORROW

Vision takes you to a land called tomorrow. I've heard tomorrow defined as a "land where 99% of all human productivity, motivation, and achievement is stored."[3] Do you ever feel as if that represents the tomorrow you're headed toward—that place where you'll be more productive, more motivated, and more accomplished? Does the tomorrow you dream of seem far away or even just out of your grasp when each passing today turns into the same today you lived yesterday? This is such a common theme in our lives that movies such as *Groundhog Day*, *50 First Dates*, *Source Code*, and *Edge of Tomorrow* have been tremendously successful! But you have to disrupt the recurring patterns of your life.

So how do you disrupt the recurring patterns of your life? How do you keep from repeating the same day over and over again? I've learned through my dealings with people, my coaching and consulting services, and my leadership studies at Oxford that success can hinge upon the types of questions we're asking. If we're asking the wrong questions, we'll get the wrong answers. Sometimes all you need to do is ask a different question. Questions are what frame your context—and if your context is wrong, your conclusions will be wrong. The difference between one season and the next is hidden in the flow of information.

Questions direct your focus and expectations—in other words, your thoughts and mind-set. When you learn the art of asking the right questions, you will get the right answers. If you've read *Commanding Your Morning*—or any of my books, for that matter—you already know that what's in your mind determines what's in your life. Whatever you think about comes about (Prov. 23:7). And although you may not realize it, your active mind is always in the process of asking some type of question. In fact, I would take that principle one step further to add that the questions you're asking fall into two categories: you're either asking "What's wrong?" or "What's possible?" The nature of the questions you ask yourself will direct your attention, your focus—and, of course, what you focus on expands. You will ultimately get more of whatever you pay the most attention to.

This is why Paul told the Ephesians, "Keep your minds thinking about whatever is true, whatever is respected, whatever is right, whatever is pure, whatever can be loved, and whatever is well thought of. If there is anything good and worth giving thanks for, think about these things" (Philippians 4:8, NLV). This is how important it is to deliberately direct your focus—and therefore why it's so important to have a clear vision. This is what makes a vision board and the practice of visualization so powerful. These tools enable you to focus your attention on what you want more of, not what you want less of—in other words, to maintain a focus on what you *want*, not what you *don't want*.

If you want more abundance, then become fixated on abundance, including the abundance you already have. An abundance mind-set "comes from appreciating all you already have and all that you already are," teaches success expert Darren Hardy. It's the attitude of gratitude, he says, that will completely shift your reality:

> We can stop the natural negative doubts that are deep inside our minds by redirecting our mind's attention and focus toward abundance and all that is possible. This simple shift can change everything about how you experience or perceive your reality. A focus on what you already have adjusts the apparatus of your mind to pay more attention to what's possible rather than what's wrong.[4]

If you operate from what you lack, you will continue to produce outcomes that match it. So stop asking "What's wrong?" and start asking "What's possible?" When you change the question, you change the lens through which you see and therefore change the future that's possible for you. Change your mental stance from a "Why me?" mentality to a "Try me!" mentality. Instead of asking why bad things happen to you, ask how you can prevent those bad things from ever happening to you again. Change your *why* into a *how*, and then ask God to give you the wisdom to walk out the answers. And, as the Bible states, when you ask, it shall be given to you (Matt. 7:7).

Try this simple experiment. Just before going to bed tonight, bow your head in prayer, ask God a "how" problem-solving question, and go to sleep. Then throughout the day tomorrow observe answers and options filling your mind.

You might not realize it, but every question you ask is emotionally charged. Just as a boat leaves a wake behind it, every question you ask leaves an emotional wake. Asking "What's wrong?" leaves a negative emotional wake. The key is to ask questions that put you

41

in a positive state of mind. Asking the right questions can change or help develop your vision, your purpose, and, in my experience, the nature of your expectations.

Change your mental stance from a "Why me?" mentality to a "Try me!" mentality.

PRACTICING THE ART OF APPRECIATIVE INQUIRY

In his 1986 doctoral dissertation Dr. David Cooperrider originated the theory of appreciative inquiry as an approach to organizational change management. Simply put, appreciative inquiry analyzes what is working well in an organization and then determines how it can do more of it. "The basic tenet of AI is that a team or an organization will grow in whichever direction that people in the organization focus their attention."[5] It proposes a methodology opposite to the old-school "fix it" model. Like doctors who focus on promoting health rather than treating disease, AI seeks to discover what people are already doing well and where they are inherently strong, rather than deconstructing their weaknesses and showcasing all the ways they've fallen short.

We can clearly see the difference in the types of questions the AI model advocates—it's an asset-driven rather than a deficit-driven approach. For example, rather than asking "What can we do to minimize customer complaints?" an appreciative question would sound more like "When have customers been most pleased with our service and what can we learn and apply from those moments of success?"[6]

This is why when it comes to your life, it is important to define the overall focus of inquiry. Rather than approaching the question of how to create a better tomorrow from a problem-solving mind-set, approach it from a solution-oriented outlook. These types of questions are rooted in your values and priorities. For example, writes Brett Steenbarger in *Forbes*, "When the implicit question is about 'What can I get done now?' we are pushed by the demands of the present. When the question is 'What will make today special?' we are pulled toward our priorities."[7] In other words, don't be limited by your current schedule or what you feel you can get done on any given day. It's more about what you are moving toward and who you are becoming in the process. I think of morning glories that shift ever so slightly in the direction of the sun and slowly open in response to its warmth.

This is what asking appreciative-type questions will help you do. They will help you position yourself in the direction of a bright tomorrow and compel you to open your awareness to the possibilities it holds.

Asking appreciative questions is a four-step process based on the "4-D Cycle" developed by Dr. Cooperrider. It asks you to first identify what is already working well—where you are already experiencing a degree of success—and with that in mind to consider what more is possible. This is where you are asked to tap into the power of your imagination and capacity to dream. With that potential future in mind, you are asked to craft a vision of those desired outcomes and, finally, determine the steps necessary to bring them to pass.

1. Discover—What's working? (Appreciating)

2. Dream—What's possible? (Imagining/envisioning)

3. Design—What should be? (Determining)

4. Deliver—What will be? (Executing/creating)

In the next sections of the book I will help you dream, design, and deliver your best possible tomorrow. But before I do, I want to help you discover what's already working well for you and appreciate the gifts you've already been given.

HOPE FOR YOUR FUTURE

Sometimes all we really need to do is wake up to all we already have. We just need to turn the lights on in the various rooms of our lives to see the beautiful furnishings, the decorated walls, the closets full of clothes, and even the array of knickknacks displayed on the shelves that we placed there because they brought a spark of joy. For most of you reading this book, you live in such abundance that it's easy to take it for granted. It's our natural proclivity to see only what's missing, what we don't yet have, or what we have not yet achieved.

I believe this is why there is an emphasis in the Bible on giving thanks. Paul told the Ephesians to "give thanks always for all things" (Eph. 5:20, MEV). In fact, in numerous places we are instructed to offer a sacrifice of thanksgiving. (See, for example, Leviticus 7:12–13; 22:29; Psalm 116:17; Amos 4:5; and Jonah 2:9.) It's an attitude of perpetual gratitude that awakens you to the abundance around you. It turns up the dimmer so you can see the blessing and favor of God working on your behalf and the opportunities He is always placing before you. More often, it's not that you lack opportunity; it's that you don't see it. You don't have eyes to see what's possible for you in every given moment. You are called by God to wake up from your slumber and metaphorically "arise from the dead"—and when you do, "Christ will give you light" (Eph. 5:14).

From the Old Testament to the New, we are urged to wake up and rise up. Isaiah urges you to wake up, arise, shine, and clothe yourself with strength (52:1; 60:1), 1 Corinthians implores you to be cognizant of right living (15:34), and Revelation commands you to awaken and strengthen whatever it is you have (3:2). There is always some good thing working on your behalf that you can strengthen if you are only awake to it.

So you need to "stop focusing on the negatives and everything that could go wrong, and start thinking of what could go right. Better yet, think of everything that already is right."[8] Be thankful that you woke up this morning. Be thankful for clothes on your back and food on your table. Be thankful for friends who became family. Be thankful for family members who are also your friends. Be thankful for your dreams and goals that have become reality in your life. Then use this positive mind-set to move you through the waters toward a brighter present and a brighter future.

This is the first buoy marking your course to tomorrow. What strengths or opportunities do you already have—even if they are seemingly insignificant—that you could make more of? Don't underestimate the powerful good that comes from stewarding well whatever little you already have, for we are told, "Whoever can be trusted with very little can also be trusted with much" (Luke 16:10, NIV). I find it interesting that we often interpret this verse from a lack mind-set—we think of the meager pickings we've been given, like a rotten potato we should turn into a stew. But I challenge you to approach this from an abundance mind-set. What are those small things that bring you great joy? When you look over your life, when were those times you felt you were able to really gain traction or capture momentum, those moments when you felt most alive or soul-fully awake? I have always loved this quote by civil rights activist Howard Thurman: "Don't ask what the world needs. Ask what makes you come alive and go do it, because what the world needs is people who have come alive."[9]

Don't sell the world short by ignoring what may seem like a quirky passion. Those are the divine desires fired by passion that God has seeded in your heart. Where your passion collides with the problems you see around you is where you'll find your purpose. Ask yourself questions that will lead you in that direction and deepen your sense of meaning and fulfillment. Instead of asking "What should I do?" ask "Why does this matter?" Always keep that bigger *why* before the smaller *what*.

Now ask yourself questions that connect you to your strengths. Think about a time when you were at your best. How can you take the qualities you brought to that moment into the present and use them to build a better tomorrow? Determine in your mind that you will approach whatever life throws your way from a place of strength. Whatever it is you need to overcome any challenge is already inside of you. In fact, you have been uniquely endowed with a specific set of strengths that will enable you to convert those challenges into opportunities.

Adversity always comes with an opportunity to develop yourself.[10] Vision will always stretch you beyond where you are and activate steep and deep learning curves. You cannot progress beyond the length and the depth of your ability to learn. The skills that you currently have must be polished, honed, and sharpened. So what are those challenges that will sharpen your skills? Or what are those capacity-building encounters you can run headlong into? This will help you define and refine what is already great about who you are and build upon it.

Life is like a ship on an ocean of opportunities. You don't have to be swept away by the currents of change if you know how to use your vision and engage your values to set your course toward tomorrow. You can then guide your vessel, allowing the winds of your passion to fill your sails of faith, moving you ever closer to the shore of your destiny. When you are confident in the type of prophetic ship you are based on your own inherent strengths, you can pull up the anchor of fear and leave the docks of doubt behind. You can then locate your north star, establish your desired direction, and head toward the shores of your longed-for destiny.

In the next section we will focus on questions that connect you with a positive image of the future. You will harness the power of your imagination and develop your ability to dream bigger than you might have thought possible before. We will dig into the mechanics of imagery and the art and science of visualization. This is the next step on the journey to creating your own epic tomorrow. "We cannot live what we cannot dream," said author Richard Paul Evans.[11] Let's start creating that dreamed-of future now. It's time to get on the road and say "Hello" to your tomorrow!

> The arduous task of intervention will give way to the speed of imagination and innovation; and instead of negation, criticism, and spiraling diagnosis, there will be discovery, dream, and design.
>
> —DAVID COOPERRIDER

> The imagination…is the very eye of faith. The soul without imagination is what an observatory would be without a telescope.
>
> —HENRY WARD BEECHER

STEP TWO

Put Yourself Where You See Yourself

If I were to wish for anything, I should not wish for wealth and power, but for the passionate sense of the potential, for the eye which, ever young and ardent, sees the possible. Pleasure disappoints, possibility never.

—SØREN KIERKEGAARD

After Lot had departed from him, the LORD said to Abram, "Lift up now your eyes, and look from the place where you are, northward and southward and eastward and westward. All the land that you see I will give to you and to your descendants forever. I will make your descendants like the dust of the earth, so that if a man could number the dust of the earth, then your descendants could also be numbered. Arise, and walk throughout the land across its length and its width, for I will give it to you." So Abram moved his tent and came and settled by the oaks of Mamre, which are in Hebron, and built an altar to the LORD there.

—GENESIS 13:14–18, MEV

CHAPTER FOUR

• • •

Dare to Dream

Martin Luther King did not say, "I have a
strategic plan." Instead, he shouted, "I have
a dream," and he created a crusade.
—UNKNOWN

Dream lofty dreams, and as you dream, so shall you
become....Dreams are the seedlings of realities.
—JAMES ALLEN

ONE OF THE most famous visionaries mentioned in the Bible was Joseph. Implementing his dream through vision and strategy was what caused Egypt to become a superpower in his day. When you have a vision, I believe it becomes your superpower that helps you surmount conditions and situations that would normally stifle your voice and bury your potential. I arrived at this theory reading about the amazing Michaela DePrince.

Born Mabinty Bangura in war-torn Sierra Leone, Michaela lost her father to rebel violence at three years old and her mother to starvation soon after. She was taken to an orphanage, where she was discriminated against because of her vitiligo—a skin condition that results in irregular pigmentation. Not long after, the orphanage came under rebel attack, and so did she. She was stabbed with a machete before a guard intervened. And then came the trek for miles as survivors fled to a distant refugee camp.

Michaela was four when she joined her American family in Cherry Hill, New Jersey. The only thing she brought with her was the cover of a magazine she found blowing across the grounds of the orphanage. It was a photo of a beautiful ballerina. She wanted to be that ballerina more than anything. Her new mother, Elaine DePrince, recognized her passion and helped her pursue her dream, and today Michaela is dancing on the world stage as a soloist with the Dutch National Ballet.[1] She has been featured in ads for Jockey and Chase Bank, has appeared alongside Beyoncé in a hit music video, and is the author of two books, one of which is being adapted into a Hollywood screenplay to be directed by Madonna.

It all began with a vision—a powerful image she held in her mind. That vision was seeded by the desire of a future possibility. That desire was rooted in a longed-for feeling of freedom and joy. And that longed-for feeling was deliberately pursued through sustained and intense focus. It was her deep-seated desire that enabled Michaela to maintain a steadfast focus on the dream she had determined to chase, no matter what people, circumstances, or perceived shortcomings told her otherwise. In the words of pioneering educator and author Marsha Sinetar, "Burning desire to be or do something gives us staying power—a reason to get up every morning or to pick ourselves up and start in again after a disappointment."[2]

THE POWER OF DESIRE

It's been almost twenty years since Jack Canfield and Mark Victor Hansen published their best seller *The Power of Focus*. It was published after their epically successful Chicken Soup for the Soul series. How the first Chicken Soup for the Soul book in the now mega-series came to be a best seller is an amazing story of focus and determination all on its own, having been turned down by every single New York publisher. As the authors were on the verge of losing heart, a small unheard-of publisher in Deerfield Beach, Florida, took an interest, and the rest is history. The *Chicken Soup for the Soul* blockbuster positioned Canfield and Hansen for the launch of their book *The Power of Focus*, which has proved to be a pioneering classic in how to harness the power of your mind to achieve your goals.

There is no doubt that focus is a powerful mental tool. As we've said, you amplify whatever it is that commands your attention—or rephrased we could say, wherever you focus your mental energy grows in its power and influence over your life. And this is precisely why it is so very important to pay attention to (otherwise known as being mindful of) what you focus on! Mindfulness has become a catchphrase in popular culture, but beyond practicing "being present" as a mental exercise, I want to direct your mind to what you deeply desire.

Similar to the law of focus, you will ultimately find whatever you look for. So what are you looking for? As Jesus asked the blind man, "What do you want Me to do for you?" (Mark 10:51). And as Mark Twain is credited with observing, "I can teach anybody how to get what they want out of life. The problem is that I can't find anybody who can tell me what they want."[3] How mindful—and yes, present—are you to the longings of your heart, your deep-seated passions, or that dreamed-of destiny you imagined for yourself as a child?

Even more powerful than focus is desire. Why? Because desire has the power to command your focus like no other force. Napoleon Hill wrote, "Strong, deeply rooted desire is the starting point of all achievement."[4] He also wrote that "Desire [is] not a *hope*! It [is] not a *wish*! It [is] a keen, pulsating desire, which transcend[s] everything else." He added, "Weak desires bring weak results, just as a small amount of fire makes a small amount of heat."[5] A contemporary of Hill, Robert Collier, said, "Plant the seed of a desire in your mind and it forms a nucleus with power to attract to itself everything needed for its fulfillment."[6] Desire is a powerful force you must learn to leverage if you are to effectively direct your focus.

THE HERO'S JOURNEY

If you're an avid film buff, you've most likely heard of the concept called the hero's journey. It is believed to be the structure of every great story, otherwise known as the monomyth: "the common template of a broad category of tales that involve a hero who goes on an adventure, and in a decisive crisis wins a victory, and then comes home changed or transformed."[7]

The study of the hero myth began in 1871 with Edward Taylor's theory that every story narrative shares a common pattern. Later, Joseph Campbell popularized the concept with the publication of his 1949 book *The Hero With a Thousand Faces*, in which he describes the basic narrative pattern: "A hero ventures forth from the world of common day into a region of supernatural wonder: fabulous forces are there encountered and a decisive victory is won: the hero comes back from this mysterious adventure with the power to bestow boons on his fellow man."[8] Campbell identified three stages of the monomyth with seventeen subsections,[9] but Hollywood screenwriter Christopher Vogler identified twelve key elements in his 2007 screenwriting guide, *The Writer's Journey: Mythic Structure for Writers*.[10] More recently Donald Miller, author of *Building a StoryBrand*, used only seven elements in his "selling with story" framework.[11] However, what I want to refer you to now is the most streamlined of all the story frameworks I've yet discovered.

Every story consists of "a character who wants something and must overcome conflict to get it."[12] According to Groundworks founder Ken Janke, who "developed Story Lab to help individuals author the story they want to live," the "want something" part of that definition is "the object of desire."[13] An object of desire could literally be an object, or it could be an idea, a feeling, an accomplishment, or even a person. Proverbs tells us that "a desire accomplished is sweet to the soul" (13:19). So what is worth chasing for you? What in your opinion would make for a worthy adventure or an epic life story? Through Story Lab, Janke helps participants identify and develop the kind of story they want their lives to tell by considering these three questions:

1. In your story what is the object of desire?

2. What does your character value?

3. What is the cause your character is willing to fight for?

By defining your core desire, your core value, and your core cause, you will be able to articulate the controlling idea of your story—somewhat like a personal mission statement.[14] A controlling idea, a desired direction, will help direct your life much like the North Star provides a fixed point sailors use to maintain a ship's bearing. So let me ask you: What is your object of desire? What obstacles are you willing to overcome to obtain it? What are you willing to fight for?

Here is the principle: If your life were turned into a movie, what would you be seeking? What kind of obstacles would you have to overcome? Would you recognize your object of desire when you found it? Is whatever it is you're chasing worth pursuing? Does the pursuit of your object of desire make a good story? More importantly, does pursuing what you desire make for a good life?[15] "We *are* desire," writes author John Eldredge. "It is the essence of the human soul, the secret of our existence....Desire fuels our search for the life we prize....Desire, both the whispers and the shouts, is the map we have been given to find the only life worth living."[16] He also notes:

> Absolutely nothing of human greatness is ever accomplished without it. Not a symphony has been written, a mountain climbed, an injustice fought, or a love sustained apart from desire. Our desire, if we will listen to it, will save us from committing soul-suicide, the sacrifice of our hearts on the altar of "getting by." The same old thing is not enough. It never will be....We abandon the most important journey of our lives when we abandon desire.[17]

Don't underestimate the power of your God-given desires. They are what God uses to lead you toward His purposes for you. Your passions were seeded into the soil of your soul before you were born (Ps. 139:13); if properly cultivated, they will bloom into beautiful fields or a grand forest blessing countless others—they will lead you into the epic story God intends your life to tell.

Today I challenge you to become the hero of your own God-given adventure story. Step up onto the bridge of your life's ship, and with the north star of your desired direction as your guide, courageously sail toward the horizon and the shore of your destiny. Meditate on these verses for a moment, and be inspired by their richness:

> Delight yourself also in the LORD, and He shall give you the desires of your heart. Commit your way to the LORD, trust also in Him, and He shall bring it to pass. He shall bring forth your righteousness as the light, and your justice as the noonday. Rest in the LORD, and wait patiently for Him; do not fret because of him who prospers in his way, because of the man who brings wicked schemes to pass.
> —PSALM 37:4–7

YOUR PROCLIVITY TO DREAM

You were born with a natural proclivity to dream. No one had to teach you how to get lost in your thoughts, to daydream or pretend or make believe. Making believe—making yourself believe something you imagine is possible—is how you're wired; it's in the divine DNA you inherited from your heavenly Father. I think in our younger years God was giving us a practice run on how to use our imaginations to prepare us for the world-changing visions He would later download into our minds. Your Creator, who has the ultimate ability to imagine and "is able to do exceedingly abundantly above all that we ask or imagine" (Eph. 3:20, MEV), delights in watching you grow your capacity to imagine. When you can imagine more, you can create more because you can believe for more to His praise and glory.

> God can do anything, you know—far more than you could ever imagine or guess or request in your wildest dreams! He does it not by pushing us around but by working within us, his Spirit deeply and gently within us. Glory to God.
>
> —EPHESIANS 3:20–21, THE MESSAGE

I am reminded again of little Mabinty Bangura, who in spite of her circumstances as an outcast orphan retained the capacity to dream—to imagine herself as a prima ballerina. She may have lost everything, but she didn't lose her ability to dream—and to dream big! Her dream was founded on a burning desire—a desire others could have told her she shouldn't have because it seemed impossible to the natural mind. But the desire remained, and so did the dream based on an image she held in her mind: the image of the prima ballerina on the cover of that magazine that so serendipitously blew across her path that day. The same magazine may have blown past a dozen other girls, but it was Mabinty who grabbed hold of it *and the dream*—or the desire—it represented.

When asked in an interview what it was about that photo that so inspired her, Michaela DePrince explained it represented a feeling she deeply longed for—the feeling of joy.[18] To her young eyes, that ballerina looked happy and free and strong and so very beautiful. As a lonely, ostracized three-year-old who felt there was no hope for her to be accepted and loved and wanted by a family, that photo represented what she hoped to one day become: accepted, worthy, and adored—and how that would make her *feel*.

Our dreams are rooted in desires, and desires are informed by feelings we long to have. It is how the fulfillment of the desire will make us feel that attracts us to it. *Desire* is partially defined as "a strong feeling,"[19] and those feelings are the natural soul state you were created to live in. They represent aspects of the kingdom and the abundant life Jesus came to give—peace, joy, and belonging (John 10:10; Rom. 14:17). So your desires are God-inspired.

I find it interesting that if you look into the etymology of the word *desire*, you will find that scholars believe its original sense was "await what the stars will bring" from the phrase *de sidere*, meaning "from the stars," which is derived from a word meaning "heavenly body."[20] So it makes sense that God is the author of the desires of your heart (Ps. 21:2). The more time you spend with Him, the more of His desires you'll have—and the more you can look to Him in faith to fulfill them knowing it is He who has placed them there (Ps. 37:4).

VISION AS A SPIRITUAL DISCIPLINE

Desire has to be accompanied by discipline for it to be translated into a reality. There is a great example of the spiritual discipline of vision in Napoleon Hill's book *Think and Grow Rich*. Many of us have never heard of him as a central figure in Edison's success; however, Napoleon Hill tells the story of Edwin Barnes, who he described as, "The man who 'thought' his way into partnership with Thomas A. Edison."[21]

Hill recounts the first meeting between Edison and Barnes:

> Mr. Edison said, "He stood there before me, looking like an ordinary tramp, but there was something in the expression of his face which conveyed the impression that he was determined to get what he had come after. I had learned, from years of experience with men, that when a man really desires a thing so deeply that he is willing to

stake his entire future on a single turn of the wheel in order to get it, he is sure to win."[22]

Hill goes on to explain that Barnes had no money and little education, and certainly no position or influence, "but he did have initiative, faith, and the will to win. With these intangible forces he made himself the number one man with the greatest inventor who ever lived."[23] Mr. Barnes had to expend effort in the face of disheartening circumstances to garner an opportunity to work in the company of Edison, and in doing so he demonstrated the power of vision to deflect discouragement and fuel discipline.

> *A dream-inspired vision undergirded by spiritual discipline has the fiery power to incinerate deterrents, doubt, disappointment, and despair.*

This is probably my favorite story from Hill's classic book that I've revisited so many times.[24] Here is how Mr. Hill explained the secret sauce to Barnes' success:

He did not say, "I will work there for a few months, and if I get no encouragement, I will quit and get a job somewhere else." He did say, "I will start anywhere. I will do anything Edison tells me to do, but before I am through, I will be his associate." He did not say, "I will keep my eyes open for another opportunity, in case I fail to get what I want in the Edison organization." He said, "There is but one thing in this world that I am determined to have, and that is a business association with Thomas A. Edison. I will burn all bridges behind me, and stake my entire future on my ability to get what I want." He left himself no possible way of retreat. He had to win or perish! That is all there is to the Barnes story of success![25]

The obstacles he faced—whether the initial lack of money or lack of transportation to get to New Jersey where the Edison organization was located or Barnes' less-than-appealing appearance that Edison readily noticed upon meeting him—were not deterrents. The spiritual discipline inspired by a clear and compelling vision allowed Barnes to move beyond the egotistic self and connect to the spiritual essence of that vision, which subsequently provided him with a deep sense of peace while traveling toward its realization. In other words, the spiritual nature of Barnes' vision infused it with transcendent meaning and certainty.

A dream-inspired vision undergirded by spiritual discipline has the fiery power to incinerate deterrents, doubt, disappointment, and despair. "Vision will get you inspired. Discipline will take you to your destination."[26]

YOUR OBJECT OF DESIRE

God created you with a purpose in mind—and the clues He has given you are the desires He has seeded in your heart. Those desires are the seeds of God's dream for you. Learn to dream with God, and get hold of His big dream for the impact you can make with your one precious life—just like so many great innovators, artists, scientists, inventors, entrepreneurs, engineers, or social justice advocates. Get hold of what more is possible with Christ. Desire more. As theologian and author Wendy Farley states, "Desire is the absurdity that holds open the infinity of possibility."[27] And in the words of Paul Vernon Buser, "Desire, like the atom, is explosive with creative force."[28]

I encourage you today to dream bigger—to take the lid off what you are able to imagine is possible for yourself. "Far too often we downsize our potential and the story God has for us," writes Charlena Ortiz, founder of Grit and Virtue. "We tend to lean on the 'someday' belief when in reality our someday is today. Dream! Map it out. Then ask yourself if the decisions you're making today align with your vision."[29]

Follow your north star, your object of desire dictated by purpose and informed by your passions and values—it will lead you to the destination you dream of. In the next chapter we will continue exploring the world of imagination and how you can leverage it to change not only your own life but the lives of so many others. Transformation is what a powerful vision is all about. The tides of history rise and fall on the boldness of its visionaries.

> The soul's hours of strong excitement are its luminous hours—its mountains of vision, from which it looks over the landscape of life with unobstructed gaze, and takes bearings for its direction.
>
> —HENRY WARD BEECHER

> The only way to be obedient to the heavenly vision is to give our utmost for God's highest, and this can only be done by continually and resolutely recalling the vision.
>
> —OSWALD CHAMBERS

• • •

CHAPTER FIVE

Reimagine Your Future

Nothing limits achievement like small
thinking; nothing expands possibilities
like unleashed imagination.
—WILLIAM ARTHUR WARD

You possess…imagination—the instrument
by which you create your world.
—NEVILLE GODDARD

DISAPPEARING AND INVISIBLE buildings sound like something
from a sci-fi thriller. But not for South Koreans, who are taking
a different approach to what they believe to be a salient feature of
skyscrapers of the future. They believe that although skyscrapers
have become iconic all over the world and many are awe-inspiring,
most skyscrapers have a tendency to obstruct beautiful views and
landscapes. The solution? The construction of a 1,476-foot-tall
building called Tower Infinity, which is designed to be "invisible."

The skyscraper will provide an unobstructed view of the sky
behind it by using an LED facade system. It's become known as an
architectural breakthrough that has opened new possibilities in the

field of architectural engineering. GDS, a California-based landscape design firm, decided it was important to innovate skyscrapers based on some other factor besides height. They pushed the architectural industry forward by proposing a structural feat that would inspire awe through "diminishing its presence" rather than the typical monolithic constructions that dominate a city's skyline.[1] Such a thing was unheard of and created a complete paradigm shift in the world of environmental design and urban aesthetics.

Vision is future focused. Envisioning the future is what Noah did. I can only imagine Noah introducing the idea of a boat that floats and has the capacity to save people from drowning in a flood caused by rain. It had never even rained before! And why would anyone in his right mind design something that had no current use? No one in previous generations had ever needed anything even remotely resembling the ark, that gargantuan contraption God commanded Noah to build. Yet with a vision, God empowered Noah to be His chosen vessel for restarting humanity—for hitting the reset button, so to speak—and Noah was able to sail safely into the future that awaited him.

When we use the insight of the unusual perception a future-focused vision gives us, we are able to see where our world in general and industries in particular can potentially go. When we do this, we pull the future toward us. As Steve Jobs, one of the great visionaries of our time, frequently stated, "If you are working on something exciting that you really care about, you don't have to be pushed. The vision pulls you."[2]

Visionaries are trendsetters. Not only are they able to look toward the horizon of possibilities, but they are also able to sail beyond it to places others fear to go. Just because something has never been done before does not mean it cannot be done now. Visionaries are individuals who are filled with faith. It takes faith in God to believe that He will empower you to do what He reveals to you as an assignment or purpose. In your prayer time ask God to help you see the things He has uniquely equipped you to accomplish. Allow God to give you an unobstructed view of the future and then pray for the wisdom, creativity, and innovative skill to craft it. Vision does not consider the present situation, conditions, availability of resources, or lack thereof—a vision only takes into account possibilities and presents them to you as plausible eventualities.

THINGS ARE NOT AS THEY APPEAR[3]

Lasting human progress and development begin within the confines of people's imagination—within the imagination of individuals who possess the faith, conviction, courage, and innovative genius not only to think outside of the proverbial box but to tinker until a new box is framed out. They disrupt industries and markets and change the trajectory of social and scientific trends. They use whatever resources are available and work until their thoughts, ideas, and dreams become a product, good, or service by taking consistent developmental steps toward its manifestation through innovation, diligence, and hard work. These are individuals who risk everything to become all that they have the potential to be. They are not defined by the status quo, social or cultural lids that are placed upon them, or even accepting life "as it is." (The saying "It is what it is" has been used by the enemy to dumb down the masses.) Instead, visionaries march to the rhythm of purpose and are propelled by potential and vision.

You do not have to accept your life as it is, nor do you have to accept your present circumstances. You can live the life of your most daring dreams. The Book of John tells the story of the man at the pool of Bethesda who had been sick and suffering for thirty-eight years. His illness rendered him unable to walk. But then Jesus came along, saw him lying there on his bed, and told him to take up his bed and walk. (See John 5:1-8.) To me, the man's bed represented the thirty-eight years he went to sleep and dreamed of a better life. But the time came when he had to stop merely dreaming; he had to stand up in faith and walk. You are not limited to only dreaming of a better life. You can put feet to those dreams by faith and walk them out beginning right here and now. It's time to rise. It's time to hoist your sails of faith and get moving toward the shore of a destiny that is even greater than you imagine.

The Book of Genesis shares many stories of the incredible power of imagination. In Genesis 13 we read where Abraham receives the following instruction from the Lord:

> Lift your eyes now and look from the place where you are—northward, southward, eastward, and westward; for all the land which you see I give to you and your descendants forever....Arise, walk in the land through its length and its width, for I give it to you.
>
> —GENESIS 13:14–17

Abraham did not physically walk through the length and width of the land at that moment. He used his imagination. God was simply giving him the opportunity to gain a clearer vision of his future in order for it to come to pass. Abraham had to take responsibility for his part by using the power of his own imagination. Where you find yourself ten years from now will be the direct result of what your mind is able to conceive is possible for you. I repeat, as I so often do, "Your feet will never take you where your mind has never been."

66

In his book *Stumbling on Happiness*, Daniel Gilbert writes:

> To see is to experience the world as it is, to remember is to experience the world as it was, but to imagine—ah, to *imagine* is to experience the world as it isn't and has never been, but as it might be. The greatest achievement of the human brain is its ability to imagine objects and episodes that do not exist in the realm of the real, and it is this ability that allows us to think about the future. As one philosopher noted, the human brain is an "anticipation machine," and "making future" is the most important thing it does.[4]

A strong, developed imagination is a great tool. It helps steer you in the right direction. It is a tremendous gift with amazing implications. It can help you remodel or even re-create your life or your world by inspiring the passion that puts wind in your sails. Imagination provides the creative fuel necessary for inventing, designing, engineering, writing, illustrating, composing, or even researching scientific theory. The creative power of imagination plays a vital role in achieving success in any field.

Stop dwelling on what you don't have at the expense of what you can have.

While imagination opens new paths to discovery and fascinating opportunities, we must be careful what we allow ourselves to imagine. The Bible tells us about "bringing every thought into captivity to the obedience of Christ" (2 Cor. 10:5). We have to harness our imagination. We must rein in the silly string of our thoughts to stay positive about our desires—otherwise we may create or attract unwanted events, situations, and people. If you do not recognize the power of your imagination and use it correctly, instead letting it run wild, your life experiences may not reflect your truest desires.

The lack of understanding of the power of imagination can be connected to the difficulties, failures, and unhappiness that many people experience. For some reason, most people are inclined to think negatively. They do not expect success. They expect the worst, and when they fail, they believe that fate is against them. When this attitude is changed—when imagination is used effectively, thereby changing expectations—then life will improve accordingly.

It is time to stop dwelling on what you don't have at the expense of what you can have. You cannot start with where you are not; you can only start from where you are and who you are right now.

THE EYE OF THE MIND

The word *imagine* means to "picture to oneself," from the Latin *imago*, meaning "image."[5] In other words, imagination is the picture of things inside your mind. It is the ability to form a mental representation of something that cannot currently be perceived with your senses. When I discuss this with my Executive Life Coaching clients, I define it as the ability to build scenes, objects, or events in the mind that have never existed. I explain that you can become whatever you desire to be if you can see it in your mind. This requires you to move from the domain of desire to the higher realm of forming the image of exactly how you want it to be in your mind's eye.

Visions are powerful spiritual motivators that provide inspiration. Leadership consultant and author Ian Wilson writes:

The power of vision derives from its ability to capture the hearts and minds of an organization's members by setting forth a goal that is both feasible and uplifting. It can reinforce the empowerment that most organizations today seek to promote. It focuses thought and action, providing both the readiness and the aim—as in "ready, aim, fire"—for strategic and tactical decisions, helping to ensure consistency in decision making. It is the star by which the organization steers.[6]

A large percentage of people think wishfully—they are wishful thinkers. They do not deliberately imagine, and therefore they do not produce the desired result. Imagination is a trigger that propels the mind into thinking more expansively. Your thoughts then begin to generate ideas capable of shifting your dreams into reality. If people in the past failed to employ their imaginative power, your cars, cell phones, and 4-D televisions would not be in existence. Everyone has the capacity to imagine, but only a few leverage it effectively.

Once again, listen to what God said concerning imagination: "And now nothing will be restrained from them, which they have imagined to do" (Gen. 11:6, BRG). We all have the imaginative capacity to cure diseases that have perplexed mankind for decades, to end world hunger, and to stop ever-increasing wealth disparities. We are at liberty to use this magnificent tool whenever we want to transform our dreams into reality and move humanity forward.

THE POTENTIAL PRINCIPLE

Vision gives you the opportunity to tap into your potential. Potential, simply put, is "dormant ability, reserved power, untapped strength, unused success, hidden talents, [and] capped capability."[7] The problems of our world often go unsolved because vast reserves of potential remain buried. Industry breakthroughs never happen because we don't understand that the very gifts needed are often only uncovered in the midst of crisis. A crisis in a family, community, industry, government, or nation has the power to unlock the potential of those facing the crisis.

Each one of us is responsible for cultivating our God-given potential. We must learn to understand our potential and use it effectively. Too often our past successes and failures prevent us from utilizing our latent potential. Success becomes an enemy when it causes us to settle for what we have, what we've done, what we've acquired, and so on. Failure becomes our enemy when it convinces us that any future success is not attainable for us simply because we failed in the past.

Do not let who you are today sabotage who you have the potential to be tomorrow. Don't believe the lie that you don't have enough or that you are not enough! Vision will give you the power to push on to the next level—and as you push, you will gain just what you need to press through to your next goal or dream. Your past is no predictor of your future. Potential demands that in the present of today you visualize the amazing person you will yet become.

Both success and failure have a start date and an expiration date, but potential is never-ending, unlimited, and eternal (Eccles. 3:11). What in the world are you waiting for when God has put the world in your heart in potential form? "Potential never has a retirement plan."[8] Potential refuses to be satisfied with last year's accomplishments or wallow in yesterday's failures. Potential can never be exhausted. Refuse to put a lid on the breadth, height, and depth of your dream and vision. Refuse to let what you are unable to do interfere with what you are able to do. What you see in the natural is not all there is. Psalms tells us, "Both the inward thought and the heart of man are deep" (64:6). You are more than meets the eye.

Myles Munroe said, "In order to realize your full potential, you must never be satisfied with your last accomplishment."[9] I know of businesspeople who stop at making thousands although they have the potential to make millions. I know others who make millions yet have the potential to make billions. I know of talented people who have the potential to be doctors but settled for being nurses. I know some amazing people who could own their own law practices but have resigned themselves to careers as legal assistants. I know others who could own their home but continue to rent—yet they are paying the same amount for rent as they would for a mortgage.

In his book *Uncover Your Potential*, Munroe writes the following to illustrate the power of potential:

> If I held a seed in my hand and asked you, "What do
> I have in my hand?" what would you say? Perhaps you
> would answer what seems to be the obvious—a seed.
> However, if you understand the nature of a seed, your
> answer would be *fact* but not *truth*. The truth is I hold a
> forest in my hand. Why? Because in every seed there is a
> tree, and in every tree there is fruit or flowers with seeds
> in them. And these seeds also have trees that have fruit
> that have seeds—that have trees that have fruit that have
> seeds, etc. In essence, *what you see is not all there is. That
> is potential. Not what is, but what could be.*[10]

Our Creator God placed the seed of each thing within itself (Gen. 1:12). He placed potential within every living thing that He created, including you. You have the seed of potential planted

71

within your DNA to do whatever God has commissioned you to do. It would be a tragedy for you not to realize the full potential that was divinely placed within you by the God who knit you together in your mother's womb (Ps. 139:13). Do not allow the anchor of fear to keep you moored in a harbor when you have the potential to be gliding across the water at full sail. Make the decision that you will not rob the world of the abilities, strengths, and talents given to you by a heavenly Father who loves to give good gifts to His children (Matt. 7:11). It is time to weigh anchor and set sail.

Make this statement aloud whenever the spirit of fear attempts to discourage you from taking action: "Now nothing will be restrained from me which I have imagined doing." When you speak this out, nothing will be restrained from you, and you will manifest God's best for your life. Imagine it, take action, and live your dream.

For years I've used the following compilation of various translations of Job 22:28 as my personal motto, and it ultimately became the impetus for my book *Commanding Your Morning*:

> Decide on a matter...
> Pronounce something to be...
> Whatever you choose to do...
> Decide and decree...
> And it shall be established for you...
> It shall be!

CHANGE THE WAY YOU THINK

Could things be the way they are because you are the way you are? What one thing can you change that can change everything? It's simple. Proverbs 23:7 says, "For as he thinks in his heart, so is he." So if you want to change, change the way you think.

So many people want to have a better life, but they continuously do the same thing over and over. So many people have dreams that they let die because chasing their dreams requires them to do something difficult or uncomfortable. It might mean they have to walk away from things that provided security, such as a job that paid the bills. It also might mean walking away from relationships or associations that no longer have capacity to carry us forward.

Never let who you are today sabotage who you could be in the future. Refuse to let your history interfere with your destiny! Don't let how you see yourself today inhibit who you have the potential to become tomorrow. Think for a change! Think of all that's possible. Think of the incredible potential you carry to affect change. Think of all those things you can do through Christ who strengthens you (Phil. 4:13)! Think of the generative power of your divinely engineered imagination and the transformational force of your innovative abilities.

Napoleon Hill pointed out that in terms of our thoughts becoming physical realities, there is no difference between destructive thoughts and constructive thoughts, between negative thoughts and positive thoughts.[11] That is why we must keep in mind what Paul wrote to the Philippians: "Whatever is true, whatever is honorable and worthy of respect, whatever is right and confirmed by God's word, whatever is pure and wholesome, whatever is lovely and brings peace, whatever is admirable and of good repute; if there is any excellence, if there is anything worthy of praise, think continually on these things [center your mind on them, and implant them in your heart]" (4:8, AMP).

We must be intentional about focusing our minds on our vision.

We must become so vision-conscious that the desire to successfully fulfill the vision drives us to create definite plans to achieve it. Why would anyone ever allow the enemy to seduce him or her into living a life of restriction when God has called us to a realm of unlimited potentiality? We have this treasure of infinite possibility—of eternity—within us (Eccles. 3:11).

LIBERATING THE MIND

The only thing holding you back from living the life of your dreams is your mind. Your mind is the mechanism that holds you captive and keeps you chained to your past—or anchored in a present you feel limited or restrained by. If you are feeling captive, oppressed, blind, or broken, Jesus came for you. He was sent by God explicitly to liberate you, to help you see past your current circumstances, to heal your heart and give you hope. He told us that God sent Him "to proclaim liberty to the captives and recovery of sight to the blind, to set at liberty those who are oppressed" (Luke 4:18). Could that be you? Or could that be an area of your life where you've struggled to break free from self-doubt, shame, guilt, or fear?

You have been called to stand fast in the liberty by which Christ made you free (Gal. 5:1), so if you feel stuck in any area, I want to help you move past it so you can position your heart to activate your greater potential. Before you can reenvision your future and act on that vision, you have to eliminate the perceived limitations rooted in your mind—those mental strongholds that keep you from moving forward. This is the focus of my book *Reclaim Your Soul*; this is such a life-transforming process, I wrote an entire book about it. Don't neglect this critical step in empowering yourself to create meaningful, lasting change—it is the key to personal resiliency. However, that is not the focus of this book, so I will only briefly walk you through a simple exercise I believe you will find helpful.

If you feel stuck due to an inability to move beyond a past experience, "your brain is subconsciously relating to it as if it's still happening right now," observe Marc and Angel Chernoff, coauthors of *Getting Back to Happy*. "It's matching patterns improperly in the present." The Chernoffs offer the following two-step solution. They suggest you first ask yourself, "What specific past experience and associated feelings do my current feelings remind me of?" Secondly, they recommend making a list of all the ways your current circumstances differ from that past experience. "Review the differences over and over again until you have them completely memorized. This can help you realize and remember that circumstances have indeed changed."[12]

Your subconscious mind forgets that your capabilities have grown. A beautiful illustration of this is found in a classic story told of how elephants are domesticated:

> Zookeepers typically strap a thin metal chain to a grown elephant's leg and then attach the other end to a small wooden peg that's hammered into the ground. The ten-foot-tall, ten-thousand-pound elephant could easily snap the chain, uproot the wooden peg, and escape to freedom with minimal effort. But it doesn't. In fact, the elephant never even tries. The world's most powerful land animal, which can uproot a tree as easily as you could break a toothpick, remains defeated by a small wooden peg and a flimsy chain.
>
> Why? Because when the elephant was a baby, its trainers used the exact same methods to domesticate it. At the time, the chain and peg were strong enough to

restrain the baby elephant. When it tried to break away, the metal chain would pull it back. Soon the baby elephant realized that trying to escape was impossible. So it stopped trying. And now that the elephant is fully grown, it sees the chain and the peg and it remembers what it learned as a baby—the chain and peg are impossible to escape. Of course this is no longer true, but it doesn't matter. It doesn't matter that the two-hundred-pound baby is now a ten-thousand-pound powerhouse. The elephant's self-limiting thoughts and beliefs prevail.[13]

We are a lot like that elephant, all grown up but conditioned by our self-imposed limitations and paradigms of lack, failure, and a just-getting-by mentality; conditioned to always think and act like followers when we are, in fact, leaders; and conditioned to fail when we are innately wired to succeed. We all have incredible power inside us because "the Spirit of Him who raised Jesus from the dead lives in [us]" (Rom. 8:11, MEV). We all have our own chains and pegs—the self-limiting beliefs that hold us back, whether they're childhood experiences, past failures, or lies we were told that we chose to believe. They act like barnacles or excess cargo or anchors intended to slow us down, weigh us down, or keep us from moving at all. But with God's help we can get rid of them and start sailing toward the horizon.

LEARN FROM THE PAST AND LET GO

To develop what's required for your ongoing transformation, growth, success, and prosperity, you must be willing to learn from your past—every setback, flop, failure, misstep, disappointment, hurt, or pain. Don't turn a blind eye; rather, consider how you might use them to your advantage as opportunities to grow. It's all about capacity building. Every struggle you face today is developing the strength you'll need tomorrow.

In my book *Prevail* I go into great detail about how you can develop your strengths in hard places. What are the lessons you have learned from past adversity that might help you now? Rather than wallowing in regret, consider how you might capitalize on those experiences. Find the advantages you can leverage to step up and rise to a greater level of expertise, authority, and influence. How has your past prepared you to be more determined, more focused, more self-disciplined, more perceptive, more generous, more resilient, or more compassionate? Shift your focus to what you have gained, learned, or accomplished through the pain and struggle.

"Forgetting those things which are behind" does not mean you can't learn from the things in your past even as you "press toward the goal" (Phil. 3:13–14). What it does mean is that you can sever the emotional attachment to the pain that accompanies the memory. Sit with it and use it as a teacher. Just as you can learn from your desires, you can also learn from what opposes them. The resistance you come up against might be trying to tell you something. Just as you need to wake up to the possibilities around you, as we talked about in chapter 3, you also need to wake up to the light God is showing you in the obstacles you encounter. It's simply a matter of awareness—of that mindfulness we've already talked about.

I think of Peter's command to "Keep awake! Watch at all times" (1 Pet. 5:8, NLV). Why? Because you have an adversary looking to create adversity in your life. The Bible says the enemy comes "to steal, and to kill, and to destroy" (John 10:10). It also says that "your adversary the devil walks about like a roaring lion, seeking whom he may devour" (1 Pet. 5:8). And why is that? Because he is trying to keep you from fulfilling your purpose. He is trying to keep you from living in the fullness of the destiny you've dreamed of. He is trying to keep you from the abundant life God wants you to have (John 10:10). Knowing that your actions today will determine your destiny tomorrow, let me ask you today: What is that good thing he is trying to keep you from accomplishing? Discern it for what it is, and stand firm: "Stand against him and be strong in your faith" (1 Pet. 5:9, NLV).

This is how you build your capacity to fulfill that vision I'm going to help you create in the next section. As much as vision casting, positivity, visualization, and affirmation have been hijacked by nonbelievers in what many call New Age circles, they are grounded in biblical truth. What New Thought advocates promote is merely a counterfeit of the spiritual laws outlined in the Bible—primarily the principles surrounding the activation of our faith. While there are some things worth gleaning from secular science and thought leaders in this arena, you must rely on the Holy Spirit to help you separate the wheat from the chaff.

Progress of any kind is often uncomfortable at first, but stretching your limits so you can build your capacity to achieve greater things is the only way to start living the life of your dreams. Nothing worthwhile comes easily. Even getting out of bed early in the morning can feel challenging. But we do it because of our anticipation for what the new day holds. We prepare for a tough job interview in the hope of a more fulfilling career; we sweat and lift weights for the reward of a more fit and healthy body; we train and endure in order to win—even if only to win "the prize of the high calling of God" (Phil. 3:14, KJV). Anything worthy of pursuing takes fortitude—and it takes faith.

In a blog post about letting go, the Chernoffs wrote:

> Far too many people are fearful of the unknown, comfy with putting in the least amount of effort, and not willing to put up with short-term pain for long-term gain....Growth and progress require discomfort. Every time you stretch your emotional, intellectual, and physical muscle groups, discomfort arises just before progress is made. In all walks of life, by committing to continuous, small uncomfortable steps forward, you are able to sidestep the biggest barrier to positive change: Fear.[14]

Remember that "For God has not given us a spirit of fear, but of power and of love and of a sound mind" (2 Tim. 1:7). Don't wait one more moment to dump the excess cargo weighing you down so you can sail straight ahead toward all that the future holds for you. Don't be tempted to drop anchor in the ocean of regret. Your best life is just on the other side of your comfort zone. Reimagine your future and determine a new destination for yourself! Learn from the past, and then get rid of anything that does not provide value on your journey to a better tomorrow.

> Today is a new day. Don't let your history interfere with your destiny! Let today be the day you stop being a victim of your circumstances and start taking action towards the life you want. You have the power and the time to shape your life. Break free from the poisonous victim mentality and embrace the truth of your greatness. You were not meant for a mundane or mediocre life!
>
> —STEVE MARABOLI

Nothing paralyzes our lives like the attitude that things can never change. We need to remind ourselves that God can change things. Outlook determines outcome. If we see only the problems, we will be defeated; but if we see the possibilities in the problems, we can have victory.

—WARREN WIERSBE

CHAPTER SIX

— • • • —

Renew Your Mind

The brain's natural state is away from
possibility, so you must consciously lean
forward toward your better life.
—ROBERT COOPER

Be transformed by the renewing of your mind.
—ROMANS 12:2

MOST OF US underestimate the power of the mind. And those of us who acknowledge it often don't quite understand it. This is why I'm especially fond of the work of my friend Caroline Leaf, who has opened the world of the mind to the many who have read her books, attended her conferences, or watched her TV program. In common, everyday language, she helps her audiences understand how the mind works and how they can "work their mind" for their own greatest good. She has brought the mysteries of neuroscience into the mainstream—and shown how God is at work not only in our hearts but also in our brains.

What takes place in the brain is a profound metaphor for what we see taking place in the world around us; our outer world and the things that occur in society and in nature are a reflection of the inner world of our thoughts. The biology of our brain is simply another testament to the power of God's Word at work in all things—power that is made effective by our faith-filled thoughts (1 Thess. 2:13). We are wired, quite literally, with the neurological capacity to catalyze any type of change we want to see in our lives—whether in relation to our healing or our happiness, or the wisdom needed to solve the world's most daunting problems.

In her book *Switch On Your Brain*, Caroline Leaf states, "Thoughts are real, physical things that occupy mental real estate. Moment by moment, every day, you are changing the structure of your brain through your thinking. When we hope, it is an activity of the mind that changes the structure of our brain in a positive and normal direction."[1] She also states:

> Our choices—the natural consequences of our thoughts and imagination—get "under the skin" of our DNA and can turn certain genes on and off, changing the structure of the neurons in our brains. So our thoughts, imagination, and choices can change the structure and function of our brains on every level.[2]

Science is proving the truth of Proverbs 23:7 that as a man thinks, so is he. There is so much we can learn from the mechanics of our brain—how we can reengineer it to serve our needs. Now there has opened up entirely new fields in neuropsychology, neurolinguistics, neuroleadership, and more[3] based on the neuroplasticity of the brain: the ability of the brain to change and reorganize itself by forming new patterns of synaptic connections.[4] What science calls "neuroplasticity" the Bible calls "renewing of your mind" (Rom. 12:2).

This is partly what the practice of visualization helps you do—it helps you renew your mind. Visualization is taking the thing you've imagined and focusing your mind, will, and emotions on that particular desired outcome in such a way that it becomes the lens through which you not only see but also engage the world around you. You intentionally shift your mind and focus your thoughts, forming new patterns of thinking. New patterns of thought produce the neuropathways that will direct you forward, producing transformation and creating a change in your awareness—or consciousness—commonly called a "paradigm shift."

Why is this so important? Because, as Brian Tracy states, "What you attract into your life is in harmony with your dominant thoughts."[5] Therefore if your dominant thoughts are negatively charged, you will attract negatively charged experiences. As Tracy simply puts it, "You are a living magnet."[6] This is why, writes modern philosopher Neville Goddard, "a change of consciousness is necessary before you can change your outer world."[7]

UPGRADE YOUR CONSCIOUSNESS

According to Goddard, "A man's consciousness is all that he thinks and desires and loves, all that he believes is true and consents to."[8] In 1952 he published his seminal classic, *The Power of Awareness*, in which he introduced the concept and practice of mentally putting yourself where you see yourself. In detail he explained how to create a present state of conscious awareness of that future self, wherein you've already become that person and are experiencing how being in that future state would *feel*. You travel through time in your mind and mentally experience that future state of being. Goddard noted the importance of assuming the *feeling* that your goal has already been attained. He wrote, "It is not what you want that you attract; you attract what you believe to be true."[9]

How you believe has a physiological effect on your brain; by changing what you believe, you are able to rewire it to serve your needs. "I was exhilarated by the new realization that I could change the character of my life by changing my *beliefs*," writes Bruce Lipton in his groundbreaking book *The Biology of Belief*. "I realized that there was a science-based path that would take me from my job as a perennial 'victim' to my new position as 'co-creator' of my destiny."[10] Your beliefs are powerful, largely because they determine how you emotionally engage with what you experience—they determine how you psycho-physiologically respond to events; in other words, how they make you feel. According to Lipton, "Our beliefs control our bodies, our minds, and thus our lives."[11]

We must wake up to our true identity
and potential in Christ!

I've always found it interesting that right in the midst of the Great Depression, Napoleon Hill wrote his classic *Think and Grow Rich*. It apparently hit a chord with readers. Now, more than eighty years after it was published, it has sold more than 100 million copies.[12] In it Hill writes, "All thoughts that have been emotionalized (given feeling) and mixed with faith, begin immediately to translate themselves into their physical equivalent or counterpart. The emotions, or the 'feeling' portion of thoughts, are the factors that give thoughts vitality, life, and action."[13]

That said, if you want to change your future circumstances,

you must first change your state of consciousness—and when you do, you will change what you believe and therefore how you feel. Paul wrote to the Romans about this same principle—your entire being is transformed when your mind is transformed (Rom. 12:2). In order for transformation to take place, the whole basis of your thoughts—your state of consciousness—must change, must be renewed. I believe this is what the Bible instructs us to do with its directive "Awake, O sleeper, rise up from the dead, and Christ will give you light" (Eph. 5:14, NLT).

Most of us are sleepwalking through life, in a comatose state like the walking dead. (I have to wonder if this is why shows and movies about zombies and a zombie apocalypse have become so popular. Are these a commentary on the state of modern society?) We must wake up to our true identity and potential in Christ! When you do, "the light will dawn in your souls and Christ the Morning Star will shine in your hearts" (2 Pet. 1:19, TLB). That light is knowledge of the truth. Where darkness represents ignorance, light represents knowledge. "Your perspective is always limited by how much you know," writes Lipton. "Expand your knowledge and you will transform your mind."[14]

ENERGY IN MOTION

Light is a form of energy. It is defined by waves of energy that radiate. When something radiates, it not only spreads but also attracts. Think of the radiance of God's glory! Think when that glory "is risen up on you," as Isaiah prophesied over the people of God, how "all nations will come to your light" (Isa. 60:1, 3, TLB). This is the same "radiant" power at work in your faith-filled thoughts and words. Alternatively, thoughts and words filled with doubt and unbelief repel the light—and in the absence of light, darkness rushes in. Darkness is defined as "a lack of illumination or an absence of visible light."[15] Simply put, where there is no light, there will be darkness.

So let's look at how that plays out when it comes to our thoughts. Quantum physics tells us that all physical reality is made up of vibrations of energy, including your thoughts. Author Peter Baksa, writing for *The Huffington Post*, explains it this way:

> Your brain is comprised of a tight network of nerve cells, all interacting with one another and generating an electrical field. This electric field is detectable with standard medical equipment. Your brain waves are simply the superposition of the multitude of electrical states being formed by your nervous system....Being an electric field, all those overlying electric wave patterns that comprise your brain waves are governed by the same equations governing the electromagnetic spectrum, light, particles, and everything else in the universe. The light seen coming from a star and the energy of your mind are one and the same type.[16]

Just as currents of electricity create electromagnetic fields—connecting the positive and negative charges—your thoughts create a similar field. Your positive thoughts attract positive attachments; your negative thoughts attract negative attachments. This is why it is so important to fill your mind with the Word of God. Your faith connects you to God, which connects you to thoughts of good, not evil (Jer. 29:11). The Scripture says, "The just shall live by faith" (Rom. 1:17; Gal. 3:11; Heb. 10:38)—that faith allows you to lift the eyes of your soul to see above the waterline in order to focus on the unlimited resources available in Him.

Whenever you have a focus on God, it drives away your fear and your doubt and your frustration and your unbelief—these are the emotions that clutter your soul and your conscious mind. The spirit of the mind, therefore, must be renewed (Rom. 12:2). We're talking about a complete metamorphosis of the natural mind so you're able to think the supernatural thoughts of God concerning your life. Your mind is magnificent machinery that has been created by God—it can be used either to attract light or to attract darkness.

Have you ever heard the phrase *mind over matter*? To me this means the thoughts of the mind have a direct effect on the brain, which is matter—the neurological impulses of your thoughts impact every facet of your life and being. This is why we read in Proverbs, "For as he thinks in his heart, so is he" (23:7). Make sure there is nothing in your heart creating a magnetic force that is driving away good and bringing bad or evil toward you (Phil. 4:8). The secret of success and prosperity in the Christian life is hidden in what we meditate on. God instructed Joshua to meditate day and night on His Word: "Only then will you prosper and succeed in all you do" (Josh. 1:8, NLT).

When you deal with the imagination—the process that takes you into the future—the mind cannot distinguish whether the intellectual impulses are being fired from past or future events; they fire as if from an eternal present that already exists. I believe this is why we are told in Ecclesiastes, "He has planted eternity in the human heart" (3:11, NLT). Because what is in you comes to you, make certain it is the "kingdom of God within you" (Luke 17:21) and not something else.

This is why your imagination is so vitally important—your thoughts and your ideas. God revealed this truth in the very first book of the Bible when He stated, "Nothing will be restrained from them, which they have imagined to do" (Gen. 11:6, KJV).

Your thoughts are going to attract the things that are dominant in your mind. A mind that is filled with faith is powerful, positive, hopeful, and peace-filled—it is cleared of the clutter of worry, doubt, fear, anxiety, offense, and so on. Therefore good is attracted to you and evil is repelled from you. See through the eyes of faith (2 Cor. 5:7). It's not what happens to you that shapes you and determines the trajectory of your life—it's your perception of what happens to you. It's the lens through which your mind views the world that shapes your reality. "We can control our lives by controlling our perceptions," observed Bruce Lipton.[17] If you can change the lens and turn it into something that is positive, the outcome—no matter what you are faced with, no matter how hard times get—can only be good because the Bible says, "All things work together for good to those who love God" (Rom. 8:28).

Not only can you change the level of your happiness, but you can change the level of every single facet of your life when you begin to understand that it's not what's happening *to* you but *within* you. David prayed, "Create in me a clean heart, O God; and renew a right spirit within me" (Ps. 51:10, KJV). When it comes to cleaning the clutter of your conscious mind, it is the work of the Holy Spirit: "When the Spirit of truth comes, he will guide you into all truth" (John 16:13, NLT); "Then you will know the truth, and the truth will set you free" (John 8:32, NIV). He is able to reveal the deep things of God (1 Cor. 2:10) and expose the things in your mind, emotions, and life that are holding you hostage. Allow Him to free you from the baggage of your past, and let bygones be bygones. You have too great a future to allow negative experiences to sabotage the goodness that God has prepared for you. Get rid of the emotional clutter clouding your mind, contaminating your soul, and skewing your perception of people and situations.

What you believe to be true or correct influences your perception of everything and everyone around you—it's like wearing tinted glasses. Your reality in your thoughts colors the perception of everything that is around you at a subconscious level. This is called confirmation bias, and it is something you can become aware of and master on a conscious level. If you want to change your experiences, take control of the experiences you're having within yourself. When you change the way you look at people and situations, the way those people and situations look will change.

I can't think of a more important truth for you to grasp hold of as you reenvision your future. When you understand that everything that is happening *to* you is revealing something that's happening *in* you, you can put yourself back at the helm of the ship of your life. As James Allen so astutely observes in his classic book *As a Man Thinketh*, "The outer conditions of a person's life will always be found to be harmoniously related to his inner state....Men do not attract that which they want, but that which they are."[18]

THE ART AND PRACTICE OF VISUALIZATION

You would be hard-pressed to find a professional athlete or top achiever in any field who does not practice visualization to elevate his or her performance. In fact, numerous studies have confirmed the profound effects of visualization, including a 1980 study of Olympic-level athletes that demonstrated those who spent the most time practicing mental imagery showed far more improvement than those who did not.[19] And many well-known celebrities, such as Will Smith, Arnold Schwarzenegger, Oprah Winfrey, and Jim Carrey, attribute their success to the practice.

What makes visualization so effective? Primarily it creates a sense in your mind of whatever you're visualizing being real, thus affecting your deeply rooted belief system—and as we've just outlined, the direction of your life follows your beliefs. "When you visualize doing something, your brain functions as if you are actually performing the task," write authors Jack Canfield and Dave Andrews. And as we stated previously, they concur "the brain doesn't distinguish between actually doing something and visualizing it."[20]

This is what makes visualization so effective. You literally create a subconscious belief that the reality you've imagined already exists—and because of the energetic force of your beliefs, your life begins to align with that imagined reality. Visualization not only influences your conscious mind, but more powerful is its impact on your subconscious—where the majority of beliefs that inform your thoughts are housed. This is where much of your life's energy emanates from.

Your energy flows wherever your mind goes. In other words, your energy follows your attention, and your attention follows your focus. So deliberately focusing your thoughts where you want your life to go targets your energy in that direction. And as we've said, energy by nature is magnetic. Even static electricity generates a magnetic force. Author Kirk Wilkinson explains: "Your visualization has energy. As you visualize your intent, you will start to notice the energy that surrounds it. Energy that leads to miracles and that will bring your vision into existence."[21] Second-century Roman Emperor Marcus Aurelius summed it up this way: "Such as thy thoughts and ordinary cogitations are, such will thy mind be in time."[22] But long before Marcus Aurelius, another ruler, King

Solomon, had already recorded some divinely imparted wisdom: "For as he thinks in his heart, so is he" (Prov. 23:7).

The power of using visualization to create new scenarios in the mind—to innovate—can be demonstrated by the experiences of Nikola Tesla, a man labeled a genius by many and well known for pioneering advances in wireless communication. He began training his powers of imagination through actively visualizing his ideas. In his autobiography, *My Inventions*, Tesla writes, "I observed to my delight that I could visualize with the greatest facility. I needed no models, drawings or experiments. I could picture them all as real in my mind." He further explains:

> I gave myself up entirely to the intense enjoyment of pic-
> turing machines and devising new forms. It was a mental
> state of happiness about as complete as I have ever known
> in life. Ideas came in an uninterrupted stream and the
> only difficulty I had was to hold them fast.[23]

I read a profound story of Air Force Colonel George Hall, who was a prisoner of war in Vietnam for seven and a half mentally and emotionally exhausting years. Every day this man played a full game of golf in his imagination. Within weeks of his release in 1973 he entered the Greater New Orleans Open and shot a seventy-six—an amazing score for a man who hadn't picked up a club in all those years.[24] This story illustrates the basic principle of harnessing your imagination—in other words, acting as if that which you perceive is real and already accomplished. "Visualize this thing that you want. See it, feel it, BELIEVE in it," wrote Robert Collier. "Make your mental blueprint, and *begin to build*!"[25] I am not talking about pretending but living and acting as if what you desire has already occurred.

"Visualizing an object or a situation, and repeating often this mental image, attracts the object or situation into our lives," write authors Jasmine Renner and Bowen Bailie. "This opens for us new, vast and fascinating opportunities."[26] Henry David Thoreau observed, "The world is but a canvas to the imagination."[27]

So while it's important to take the limits off of what you're able to imagine, the process of visualization is what enables you to focus your attention on a particular outcome—on a specific feeling of that desired future state. It is the focusing of the mind's eye that is so very powerful. This requires you to develop the muscle of your attention. Your energy follows your attention, and your attention follows your focus. "Energy flows where focus goes," quips Tony Robbins. Dilute your focus, and you dilute your power.

This truth was beautifully summarized by Neville Goddard: "Attention is forceful in proportion to the narrowness of its focus.... For an idea is endowed with power in proportion to the degree of attention fixed on it.... The power of attention is the measure of your inner force."[28]

> All progress depends on an increase of attention. The ideas which impel you to action are those which dominate the consciousness, those which possess the attention.... When you set out to master the movements of your attention, which must be done if you would successfully alter the course of observed events, it is then you realize how little control you exercise over your imagination and how much it is dominated by sensory impressions and by a drifting on the tides of idle moods.... Imagination is able to do anything, but only according to the internal direction of your attention.... Sooner or later you will

awaken in yourself a center of power and become conscious of your greater self, the real you.[29]

"The great secret," wrote Goddard, "is a controlled imagination and a well-sustained attention firmly and repeatedly focused on the feeling of the wish fulfilled until it fills the mind and crowds all other ideas out of consciousness."[30] The goal here is to think "from" rather than "of" any given ideal.

It is with these foundational truths firmly in mind that we will proceed into the next section. This is where I will show you how to write your own history. You will be equipped with a map and a compass that will enable you to take the helm of the ship of your life and cast off toward the wide-open seas of your destiny.

In the next section I will lead you through crafting a powerful vision for your life. I'll show you what makes for a "magnetic" vision board. However, while a vision board can be a powerful tool, it is the *practice* of visualization that makes that tool effective—the key word here being *practice*.

> Focus on your dream and do everything in your power! You have the power to change your life circumstances.
> —NICK VUJICIC

> When you attain control of the internal direction of your attention, you will no longer stand in shallow water but will launch out into the deep of life.
> —NEVILLE GODDARD

STEP THREE

Write Your Own History

Live the story as you write it.
—NICK VUJICIC

The visible world is sustained by the invisible...by
the beautiful visions of solitary dreamers. Humanity
cannot forget its dreamers; it cannot let their ideals
fade and die; it lives in them; it knows them as
the *realities* which it shall one day see and know.
—JAMES ALLEN

• • •

CHAPTER SEVEN

Awake to Your Divine Destiny

Your vision will become clear only when you
can look into your own heart. Who looks
outside dreams; who looks inside awakens.
—CARL JUNG

The empires of the future are empires of the mind.
—WINSTON CHURCHILL

DURING THE HEIGHT of the Second World War, the last hope
of the free world was Britain's prime minister, Sir Winston
Churchill. He was an unlikely candidate for the position, but he
believed in the power of his vision combined with the providential
hand of God in his life.

Many are unaware of Churchill's unwavering faith in God—
and that it was because of this faith he did not waver as he stood
against Hitler's onslaught in our world's darkest hour. In their
book, *God and Churchill*, his great-grandson Jonathan Sandys and
coauthor Wallace Henley document this great leader's sense of

divine destiny. He was only sixteen when he remarked to a friend, "This country will be subjected somehow, to a tremendous invasion...I shall be in command of the defences of London....It will fall to me to save the Capital, to save the Empire."[1] Five years after Churchill was appointed prime minister, at seventy years of age, he was hailed the world over as the person who saved modern civilization from disaster.

"Churchill believed in 'divine destiny,'" explained Sandys in an interview. "And that's why in 1940, though severely outnumbered, like the Israelites in the book of Deuteronomy facing the overwhelmingly strong armies across the Jordan, he stepped forward and accepted the responsibility of leadership, while others, equally ambitious, refused the honor due to their lack of faith in the possibility of a general victory."[2] What caused Churchill to have that sense of divine destiny? I believe it was his faith in a loving God who was actively ordering his steps—just as he'd read many times in Psalm 37:23 (having read through the entire Bible sixteen times, as reported by his official biographer, Sir Martin Gilbert[3]). He had God's Word on it: "The steps of a good man are ordered by the LORD, and He delights in his way."

> One evening while walking from St. James' Park to Downing Street, the Luftwaffe attacked and a large explosion was heard very close-by. Thompson [His bodyguard] was very concerned for Churchill's safety. Great-Grandpapa just shrugged the danger off. Pointing to the sky he told his trusted bodyguard, "There is someone looking after me besides you....I have a mission to perform and that person intends to see it is performed."[4]

Churchill knew that the task of winning the war was beyond mere human capability. With France—the last bastion of mainland Europe—poised to fall, Britain was left alone to fend off the Third Reich. Churchill was confident in the faithfulness of a sovereign God who would not allow such evil to prevail. It was in the trenches of the First World War that he wrote in a letter, "One must yield oneself simply and naturally...and trust in God."[5] And in May of 1940, in his first wartime broadcast as prime minister, he declared, "As the will of God is in Heaven, even so let it be," quoting from 1 Maccabees 3:58–60.[6]

How desperately the world today needs leaders with Churchill's faith and vision. Could it be that you've been put on the earth at this time in history to oppose a great evil—to stand in faith as a bastion of light and hope during a dark hour? Could you be like Esther, positioned in a certain place "for such a time as this" (Esther 4:14)? Could God—*and the world*—be waiting for you to wake up to your divine destiny?

THE FORCE OF VISION

Writing a vision for your life starts with the understanding of a simple truth: that nothing happens unless someone makes it happen. While most people sit waiting for someone else to make their lives work, you are now embarking on the journey of your life by writing your own history. There is plenty of time to focus and refine your vision, but now is the time to think broadly as you begin to ponder the question "Where do I see myself at the end of this year, five years from now, ten years from now, and even at the end of my life?" Let your vision expand to match the scope of your dreams!

But don't neglect the level of faith required to see it through.

If you want to live the life of your dreams, to truly accomplish your goals and maximize your potential, you must take 100 percent responsibility for developing your faith; you'll have to stop blaming others, pointing fingers, or making excuses as to why you don't accomplish a specific goal. It means you must take ownership of every outcome—roll with the punches and get up again! "The godly may trip seven times, but they will get up again" (Prov. 24:16, NLT). You must develop the fortitude to persevere through the opposition and press on regardless of the challenges you encounter. In the famous words of Winston Churchill, "Never give in, never give in, never, never, never—in nothing, great or small, large or petty—never give in except to convictions of honour and good sense."[7] That means no more excuses. When you feel your fallen nature tempt you to excuse yourself from a great but difficult higher call—just say no. That's only your flesh talking, not the Spirit of God—for you can do all things through Christ who strengthens you (Phil. 4:13). Grab hold of the big vision God has seeded in your heart, and take responsibility for cultivating and stewarding it. You alone are the master of your fate, "the captain of [your] soul,"[8] as is so often quoted.

Taking charge of your life can start here and now. You can begin by putting thought to paper. Writing out your vision is an extraordinarily powerful exercise. If you do nothing else, do that one thing. If you read no further, stop now and write out the vision you've had stirring in your soul that perhaps until now you've disregarded. Put words to it. The simple act of articulating a dreamed-of future or idea or desire that you've been able to imagine or envision or see in your mind's eye will put it into motion; the sheer force of putting words to paper is like giving it legs to stand on. It is bringing it from the eternal realm of your soul into the temporal now—just as does forming your internal longings into faith-filled prayers. Words of any kind are a powerful spiritual force, so harness their power to serve your greatest good.

Without vision the soul has no hope, imagination has no outlet, and innovation has no future.

The act of writing out that which you picture in your mind is so important God made it a command:

> Write this. Write what you see. Write it out in big block letters so that it can be read on the run. This vision-message is a witness pointing to what's coming. It aches for the coming—it can hardly wait! And it doesn't lie. If it seems slow in coming, wait. It's on its way. It will come right on time.
>
> —Habakkuk 2:2–3, The Message

Our world needs more visionaries. Helen Keller said that having sight but no vision is worse than being blind.[9] Sight is a function of the eyes and perceives things as they are, but vision is a function of the mind and sees things as they could be. Without vision the soul has no hope, imagination has no outlet, and innovation has no future. Humanity is diminished as dreams fade. God gives His people vision as a spiritual map to provide individuals with internal direction for their lives, and nations with direction for their citizens. Vision and faith are birthed from the same womb—both give us the ability to see the future and grab hold of it in the present.

A DESTINY IS FORGED

When we think of visionaries, we don't typically look to teenage girls living in the Third World. However, Malala Yousafzai was not your typical teenager when she began arousing international attention regarding educational injustices in her native Pakistan.

Malala Yousafzai grew up in the Swat Valley in a household that prized education. But when the Taliban banned girls from attending school, her dream of a higher education disintegrated. When the Taliban began attacking girls schools in the Swat Valley, it struck terror in the hearts of most of the girls. But not Malala, who at only eleven years old refused to stop attending school. She even gave a speech titled "How Dare the Taliban Take Away My Basic Right to Education?" She was determined to press on even in the face of violent opposition. Fueled by passion and vision, she started to write about her life online, and the blog soon went viral. Malala began to speak out using her true identity on radio, on TV, and to journalists worldwide—to anyone who would listen. Her vision was now spreading like wildfire and garnered the attention of millions.

On October 9, 2012, fifteen-year-old Malala and two other young women were shot by a Taliban gunman in an assassination attempt. This only drew more media attention, captivating the world as it rallied in concern and prayer for her recovery. On October 15, 2012, the day that Malala arrived in the UK for medical treatment, UN Special Envoy for Global Education Gordon Brown, the former British prime minister, launched an international petition in Malala's name. Not only did she recover under the watchful eye of a global audience, but she is now an international spokesperson, best-selling author, and the youngest recipient of the Nobel Peace Prize. She was featured in *Time* magazine as one of the world's most influential people three years in a row.[10]

Malala was not the only young girl to embrace a world-disrupting vision. Another remarkable example is found in Mary, the mother of Jesus. As a teenager, Mary received the news from the angel Gabriel that she would carry the Messiah. The news had the potential to ruin her standing in the community and destroy her family; however, Mary chose instead to embrace God's vision with faith and courage as she exclaimed, "Let it be to me according to your word" (Luke 1:38).

Mary decided to accept this weighty assignment and successfully ran with the vision even as impossible as it seemed. She spent months preparing for the arrival of her first child. However, unforeseen events complicated her plans. Caesar Augustus decreed a census, requiring everyone to register in their hometown. This prompted Joseph to take Mary, who was in her ninth month of pregnancy, on a ninety-mile journey that took days, perhaps with Mary riding on the back of a donkey (can you say uncomfortable!), to a town so crowded that only a stable was available for her to lie down in and give birth! We can imagine Mary pouring her heart out to God in these moments, pledging to remain faithful to the vision, trusting that He would care for her and her baby.

What about you?

We all encounter challenges, opposition, and setbacks in life. When these things happen to you, do you turn bitter, blaming God? Or do you remain allegiant to the vision? Doing so is the key to giving birth to the vision God has conceived in you.

A REALITY YET UNBORN TO TIME

In the TV series *The Men Who Built America*, the director helps us conclude that we could never think of the United States of America being the superpower it is today if not for visionaries such as Rockefeller, Carnegie, Vanderbilt, Morgan, Ford, and others. They were men who sculpted the present until it looked like the future they envisioned. They defied time and stretched their minds, built capacity within their employees, and pushed the envelope of their industries until they mirrored what they believed was possible. Their ideas became the precursors to the realities we now take for granted. From the light bulb to the library, from cars to cartoons, from airplanes to air-conditioned homes, they each began with a "what if" that ended in a breakthrough of innovation that continues to fuel our global economy.

Vision is the precursor of innovation. As imaginer Walt Disney is quoted as saying, "We keep moving forward, opening up new doors and doing new things, because we're curious...and curiosity keeps leading us down new paths."[11] Vision is a powerful motivator. A dynamic vision causes everyone who hears about it either to want to get involved or pursue a vision of their own.

Newton's first law of motion states that an object at rest will remain at rest until an external force acts upon it. Vision acts as an external force to propel one into the motion of pursuing something. How you picture your life unfolding affects how it will unfold. It affects how you will live, love, grow, succeed, and prosper in life. If that which you gaze upon elicits awe and wonder, it will be replicated until you are living an awe- and wonder-filled life. If, however, what you focus on produces fear and dread, then you will experience a fear- and dread-filled life. Your life can be changed by whatever you dare to focus on or envision.

A vision is the great equalizer. It is a perpetual and dynamic resource for everyone to access and gives us the freedom to form the end results that can revolutionize the world. Vision does not consider current skills, education, or training, so don't second-guess your ability to fulfill your vision. If God gave it to you, He will also give you the opportunity to gain the experience you need to bring it to pass. Experience comes when you exercise your will to accomplish something, no matter how massive, daunting, or impossible it may seem. A vision will help you to overcome the seemingly insurmountable.

A vision is God's plan revealed to man. (See, for example, Exodus 25:9, 40; Hebrews 8:5; 1 Chronicles 28:11–12; Jeremiah 29:11.) It is a heavenly pattern given to a person who causes it to become a reality. As I mentioned earlier, ideas are spiritual entities, and the spirit realm is actually the causal realm. Therefore when you embark upon the task of writing your personal vision, you are actually tapping into a prophetic realm. Visions are spiritual realities that point man to the existence of God.

Let me remind you that gaining a vision for your life is a spiritual discipline. A vision will bring clarity to your call and purpose. It will dictate the goals you set and bring meaning and purpose to your life, causing you to become a force to be reckoned with. Vision has the power to separate you from those who do not have the capacity for where you are going. Pursuing your vision will take you to new levels of anointing. You must have a clear vision before your ministry, life, or business can experience prosperity, growth, victory, or breakthroughs into new realms of influence. A vision helps you say no to the wrong opportunities and people so you can say yes to the right ones. It also helps you identify and manage available resources to increase the probability of your success and prosperity.

A vision is God's appeal to you to stir up latent gifts, abilities, and talents so that you prepare yourself for their actualization. Your vision should vividly describe how you see your future unfolding. Vision empowers you because it focuses your attention—and therefore your intention—on all that's possible rather than all that's wrong. It's the internal force you can use to direct your own energy field; think of yourself as the superhero of your own epic story endowed with the supernatural ability to manipulate energy—some are able to create powerful gusts of wind with a wave of their hand, others generate fire, and others make waves. I've come to believe that the stories we're most attracted to are metaphors for spiritual truth—from fairy tales to adventure movies.

WAKE UP TO GOD AT WORK IN YOU

It's time to wake up. It's time to cast off the lines, weigh anchor, and raise the sails of faith that will move you toward your destiny! Nothing good happens when you never leave the harbor. Grab hold of God's promises, and sail toward the shoreline of your destiny, holding firmly to the vision He's given you as a map. Have faith that your vision—that hope you've imagined for your life of what you could do or contribute or one day become—has been placed there by God. Do you believe the vision impressed upon a young Winston Churchill was of God? Do you believe the vision that stirred in Malala's heart was of God? How about the vision Mary held on to when circumstances became difficult? "Mary treasured up all these things and pondered them in her heart" (Luke 2:19, NIV).

As a son or daughter of God, do you believe you are less favored than these? The Bible tells us that in Christ we are all favored—more specifically, that God the Father does not show favoritism (Rom. 2:11). I challenge you to speak up and say to your Father in heaven, who can do all things, "I am willing to be used of the Lord. Let it happen to me as you have said" (Luke 1:37–38, NLV).

So I ask you today, What is God saying to you? What are you hearing when you press in to heaven and listen for His voice? What is the Holy Spirit whispering to your spirit about what more He believes you're capable of? What is He laying on your heart as you look at the world around you? Whom has He placed in your path? What opportunities are you not seeing because you're not looking? Open your eyes to what God is allowing to enter your spheres of influence; open your ears to hear the needs around you in light of your gifts and abilities. What more could you be doing to build your capacity in order to maximize your potential?

This is why you need a vision. And it is why I've written this book. I want to help you write the vision and "make it plain" so you can run with it (Hab. 2:2)! To that end, I will be walking you through the practical steps you can take to make it plain—as in clear, specific, and detailed steps—in the following chapter. This will be the map you can use to direct you toward the future you've dreamed of. Now it's time to do the work of writing out the travel details of that dream destination!

> Your Vision is the promise of what you shall one day be;
> your Ideal is the prophecy of what you shall at last unveil.
> —JAMES ALLEN

> Here is a man out at sea. He has a chart, and that chart,
> if well studied, will, with the help of the compass, guide
> him to his journey's end.
> —CHARLES SPURGEON

• • •

CHAPTER EIGHT

Find Your Life Compass

Let your heart be your compass, your mind your map,
your soul your guide...and you will never get lost.
—RITU GHATOUREY

Conscience is a man's compass.
—VINCENT VAN GOGH

ONE OF THE most significant navigational tools ever invented was the magnetic compass. Even if you have a map, you won't be able to navigate without the needle of a compass pointing north. You must know where you are relative to the direction you want to go. A compass is how you orient yourself in relation to your map.

I find it interesting that over two thousand years ago, a magnetized mineral called lodestone was used to point the needle of a compass northward. Historians believe that between 300 and 200 BC the Han Dynasty in China discovered how to magnetize the needle of a compass, and later the Song Dynasty in the eleventh century understood its value in navigation. It wasn't until the early thirteenth century that this type of compass was used by

Europeans.[1] And without a compass Christopher Columbus would not have put America quite literally on the map.

I've often challenged my readers to become the Christopher Columbus of their own lives and futures and not to see rejection from the perspective of something being inherently wrong with them. Rejection is redirection. It simply means that a certain person, relationship, organization, corporation, community, or country does not have the capacity for what you are carrying. Through my books and programs I've endeavored to provide all kinds of tools to enable people to steer their lives in the direction of their most promising destiny.[2] One of the most powerful methods I've discovered is to create a personal compass that clarifies your vision in twelve key areas. We've already talked about the importance of a vision being both specific and clearly articulated in writing. As we've said, the narrower the focus, the stronger the magnetic pull.

Lodestone is one of very few minerals that are naturally magnetized. The word *lodestone* is a Middle English term meaning way-stone, derived from the Old English *lode*, meaning "way, journey, course."[3] Lodestone is a stone that leads the way. A metaphorical leading stone based on your intrinsic values will direct you to the north star of your desires. It will help you cut away the negative noise and clutter of distraction we discussed in earlier chapters. Establishing your personal compass is critical to keeping you pointed in the direction of your dreams. John C. Maxwell said, "Until I understand where I am, I can't get to where I am going. This is the value of a compass.... It's that little nudge that tells us if we are on the right path to fulfilling our potential, or on the wrong path wasting energy traveling somewhere we don't need to go."[4]

Author Idowu Koyenikan concurs: "A highly developed values

system is like a compass. It serves as a guide to point you in the right direction when you are lost."[5] You can only start any journey from where you are, so even if you feel lost, from this point forward in your life you can grab hold of the helm, hoist the sails, and begin living each day sailing toward the grander vision you've always held in your heart for yourself and your future.

TWELVE DEGREES OF FREEDOM

I've always been fascinated by the work and writing of Buckminster Fuller. Many hail him as a twentieth-century renaissance man—a celebrated architect, systems theorist, author, designer, philosopher, and inventor. He wrote and lectured right up until he passed away in 1983 at nearly eighty-eight years of age. In a book published that year he said of himself, "I am confident that the only thing important about me is that I am an average healthy human. I am also a living case history of a thoroughly documented, half-century, search-and-research project designed to discover what, if anything, an unknown, moneyless individual...might be able to do effectively on behalf of all humanity that could not be accomplished by great nations, great religions or private enterprise, no matter how rich or powerfully armed."[6] He considered himself just an ordinary individual, yet he left an enduring mark in the fields of science, literature, and architectural design.

Fuller was a true savant. He was expelled from Harvard twice and had a reputation for bucking the system, yet he was awarded twenty-eight US patents, multiple honorary doctorates, and the Presidential Medal of Freedom. It was Fuller who first wrote about what he called "twelve degrees of freedom" in his book *Synergetics: Explorations in the Geometry of Thinking*. "The 12 universal degrees of freedom," Fuller explained, "govern the external and internal motions of all independent systems in the Universe."[7] A degree of freedom is commonly defined as "an independent parameter that is necessary to characterize the state of a physical system."[8] Degrees of freedom are also sometimes referred to as "dimensions." In general, a degree—or dimension—of freedom may be "any useful property that is not dependent on other variables."[9] Fuller referred to these as "fundamental transformation freedoms" and through a series of experiments discovered there are "twelve alternate ways in which nature can behave most economically upon each and every energy-event occurrence."[10]

According to archivist Greg Watson, "Fuller was the first designer in history to understand a structure as pattern comprised entirely of energy and information."[11] Regarding those patterns of energy, "we find that in the 12 degrees of freedom," Fuller wrote, "the freedoms are all equal and they are all realizable with equal 'minimum effort.'"[12] Regarding potential futures, Fuller observed, "Experience is inherently omnidirectional; ergo, there is not just one 'other.' There are always at least twelve 'others.'"[13]

I only reference Fuller's twelve degrees of freedom (or we could say dimensions of freedom) as a metaphorical representation of not only the multiplicity of futures that are possible for you—but also how you can create a synergy around the twelve key areas I will be outlining below. In writing about Fuller's work, Watson references "the incredible potential each individual possesses to affect change," which he attributes to the "transformative power of synergy—coordinated/combined actions leading to...capacities that are orders of magnitude greater than the sum of each individual contribution."[14]

Every morning you awaken to a world of unlimited potentialities. Your vision is like a divine GPS that guides you in your decision-making process, especially since you often have a plethora of options and opportunities available to you. Writing a vision for your life can be tedious, but it is rewarding. You might consider the twelve areas we will be exploring as your own "dimensions of freedom." These will provide the twelve directional points on your life compass. When combined, it is my prayer that these will enable you to take coordinated action leading to greater capacities. In the remainder of this chapter we will systematically build out each of these twelve degrees of focus to firmly establish your own personal compass. Together they will form the basis of a total-life vision that will provide the foundation for healthy, holistic growth.

YOUR LIFE'S COMPASS

Just as a compass needs to be accurately calibrated to magnetic north in order to work properly, your life's compass needs to be accurately calibrated to the Word of God and what the Holy Spirit shows you for you to truly fulfill your God-given potential and sail safely to the shoreline of your destiny. Max Lucado wrote, "Understanding the purpose of the Bible is like setting the compass in the right direction. Calibrate it correctly and you'll journey safely. But fail to set it, and who knows where you'll end up."[15]

Isaiah 30:21 says, "Your ears shall hear a word behind you, saying, 'This *is* the way, walk in it,' whenever you turn to the right hand or whenever you turn to the left." And Isaiah 48:17 says, "Thus says the LORD, your Redeemer, the Holy One of Israel: 'I am the LORD your God, who teaches you to profit, who leads you by the way you should go.'" In order to keep the ship of your life from veering off course, you need to make sure your compass is correctly set so the Lord can lead you in the way you should go. Calibrating your compass to anything other than the Word of God and the leading of the Holy Spirit is the recipe for a shipwreck.

With that in mind, I want to help you experience how all of these areas work together. As Mr. Fuller said, your life is "inherently omnidirectional." This is why it's important to think holistically and multidimensionally. In the rest of this chapter you will put all the parts together into a dynamic whole—and create a visual showing how far greater is the sum than each individual part. From there you will be able to establish clear and attainable daily, weekly, monthly, and annual objectives that will propel you toward that desired end.

Be gentle with yourself—your initial vision for each area doesn't have to be perfect. This is a work in progress! Focus instead on opening your heart and mind to your own potential. Let yourself dream. And then, as you write, be as specific as possible. Dream big, but focus on the details. Do not edit or try to figure out how you are going to do the things you have written. Focus and work on one category at a time. Review the questions and then close your eyes. Let the Spirit of God guide your spirit and ignite your imagination. Listen for the voice behind you saying, "This is the way." Think deeply; dream expansively.

Calibrating your compass to anything other than the Word of God and the leading of the Holy Spirit is the recipe for a shipwreck.

Below each category is a series of prompts you can ponder as you begin to write your vision for that area—they are just a few suggestions to get you started. By no means limit your imagination only to what I've included here. As you consider each area, keep your most deeply held values in mind. What is important? What are your priorities? What have you not considered is possible before? How do you want to be known or remembered in that area? Be sure to write in the present tense, and whatever you write should be asset-driven rather than deficit-driven. That means instead of saying, for example, you don't want to be in debt or overweight, write that you are prospering and in top physical form. You get the idea.

So let's get started. I am limited in how much information I am able to give you here, but to delve deeper into these twelve areas, please visit www.trimminternational.com or www.trimmcoaching .com for a more in-depth study. For now, find a quiet place to settle in and focus your thoughts on the following. Write down whatever positive images come to mind:

1. Your Personal Brand

Are you clear about your personal strengths and how you add value? How well do you understand the needs, wants, and desires of those you want to influence?

Society craves larger-than-life figures—people who stand out from the crowd, defy the odds, and accomplish great things. Never be afraid of the qualities that set you apart and draw attention to you. People quickly grow tired of boring. Court and create tension by conducting your own SWOT analysis (strengths, weaknesses, opportunities, and threats). If you want to attract success and prosperity, you must make your personal brand attractive. What is a personal brand? Your personal brand is people's perception of and emotional attachment to the image that comes to their minds when they think of you.

- What are your greatest strengths? What are you really good at doing?

- List three qualities that make you unique.

- What drives and motivates you?

- What are your likes and dislikes?

- What is your personality type?[16]

- Describe your temperament and behavioral tendencies.

- List three people you really admire, and explain why.

- Who are your closest associates, and what do their lives speak about you?

- What kind of impact do you want to have? What do you want to be known for?

- What's your promise to the world, your community, your profession, your family?

- What's your value-adding proposition?

- What do you stand for?

2. Companionship/Marriage

Are you in a fulfilling relationship? Do you feel loved? How often are you expressing love to that one person whom you love most?

- What would an ideal relationship look and feel like?

- How might that relationship look after twenty, thirty, forty years?

- What is your love language? Your communication style or preference?

- What is the ideal dynamic of your relationship? (What do you expect from your spouse?)

- What type of person do you want to grow old with?

- Describe your ideal date night.

- Describe the things needed to keep your marriage healthy.

- What mutual hobbies and interests do you have?

- What goals do you have together (especially after your children leave home)?

- If you are not currently married, when will you be married, in what month of what year?

- Will your wedding take place at a chapel, church, synagogue, park, or beach? What do your rings look like?

- How many people are in the wedding? What colors are they wearing? Describe the bridesmaids' and groomsmen's attire.

- Where are you going on your honeymoon?

3. Family (immediate and extended)

How often do you enjoy quality time with both your immediate and extended family? Do you feel loved and supported? How loving and supportive are you?

- What are your favorite family traditions?

- What traditions will you pass down?

- Describe your family values.

- Describe your family's heritage.

- Describe your family's legacy.

- What type of inheritance will you leave?

4. Personal Growth and Development

How much do you invest in your growth and development? Have you made learning and trying new things a priority?

- What types of close relationships do you need to develop?

- What are your educational goals? What is your lifelong learning plan?

- How do you intend to continually enrich your life?

- What books would you like to read or add to your library?

- What types of workshops, conferences, or credentials would you find beneficial?

- What do you want to own?

- What do you want to accomplish?

- Write your Bucket List (101 things you want to accomplish before you die).

- Who are your mentors?

- Who are your coaches?

5. Career/Calling

How satisfied are you with your career or the types of roles you play? Do you feel you're making progress in the areas you've felt called to explore or pursue?

- Describe what you would do if you knew you wouldn't fail.

- What is your ultimate dream job?

- What is the industry you really want to work in?

- What would you like to have achieved?

- What would you do even if you didn't get paid for it?

- What does your ideal career look like? Do you work from home? Do you enjoy being around people every day? Do you love being "on the road"?

- Describe in detail your professional career path.

- What are the steps you need to take to get there?

6. Friends/Colleagues

How satisfying are your social relationships? Do you find the support you need among your friends and colleagues? Do you offer the kind of support you feel you should?

- What kind of close relationships do you need to develop?

- Do you have a mastermind group (a peer group for brainstorming, mentoring, and support)? If so, who are those people?

- What does your support system look like?

- Whom do you value more than anyone else?

- Who values you the most?

- Whom would you like to impress more than anyone else?

- Who holds you accountable for your decisions?

- What relationships undergird you? What relationships have encouraged your gifts to flourish?

- Who challenges you with next-level thinking?

- In whom can you confide?

7. Networks/Alliances/Partnerships

Are you connected to the types of networks or alliances that could propel you forward in your field? What types of strategic partnerships are you cultivating?

- Are you a member of any professional groups or associations?

- Are you consistently being exposed to new networking opportunities?

- Who are your legal and tax advisors?

- How do your banking and financial-planning relationships look?

- Describe your key business relationships.

8. Recreation and Renewal

Do you make time for fun on a regular basis? Do you schedule time every day for rest and renewal?

- How do you have fun?

- What are those hobbies or other creative endeavors you've always wanted to explore?

- Describe your dream vacation.

- What do you do to refresh your soul on a weekly basis?

- How do you get rid of stress?

- How do you plan to reinvent—as in *re-create*—yourself?

- Whom do you enjoy spending time with?

9. Spiritual Growth and Development

How actively do you pursue your own spiritual development? Are you connected with a community that helps you grow spiritually?

- Do you spend time reading and studying the Word of God?

- Do you have a pastor or priest that provides you with spiritual guidance?

- Do you take regular "me moments"?

- Do you engage in regular character-development activities?

- What steps will you take in order to live more authentically?

- How might you find greater fulfillment by giving back?

- What would your ideal Sabbath look like?

- Describe spiritually enriching moments you've built into your daily routine, such as prayer, meditation, and worship.

10. Financial Stability

Do you earn enough to both meet your current needs and save for the future? Do you have a budget and an investment plan? How about a will?

- Imagine all of your financial needs and goals are met. What does that look *and feel* like?

- How were you able to achieve that?

- What would a workable budget look like? Do you
  need to make some revisions to your current one?
  (Or create one?)

- Describe your retirement plan. How much do you
  want to retire with?

- Describe your saving and investment plan.

- How do you plan to underwrite your vision?

- Describe your investments and assets, including
  intellectual property, real estate, and other
  portfolios.

11. Health, Wellness, and Fitness

Do you feel satisfied with your level of fitness? How would
you rate your eating and exercise habits—or your level of energy
throughout the day?

- What would an ideal fitness program look like for
  you? What would you do and when?

- What would an ideal eating pattern or nutrition
  lifestyle look like for you?

- If you were always getting adequate rest, how
  would that routine look? What time would you go
  to bed? What time would you get out of bed? How
  would it feel?

- What is your ideal weight?

- How do you eliminate stress?

- Do you live a balanced emotional, professional, and social life?

- What is your nutrition and supplement strategy?

- What is your mental and emotional health strategy?

- What is your physical health and medical checkup strategy?

12. Legacy

How satisfied are you with the mark you're leaving on the world, or what you're leaving behind for the people or causes you care about?

- What kind of impact do you want to have?

- How will the next generation remember you?

- Who will carry on your work?

- What industry will you influence?

- What kind of inheritance do you want to leave your children?

- How will the world know you were here?

- What are the ripples you want the pebble of your life to leave?

CULTIVATE CREATIVE TENSION

Now that you have developed the twelve points of your compass, practice focusing on those positive images you've created. Creative tension is the result of both clearly visualizing where you want to be (your vision) and being honest about your current reality. The gap between vision and reality creates a natural tension that inspires action. Author Peter Senge observes, "Creative tension can be resolved in two basic ways: by raising current reality toward the vision, or by lowering the vision toward current reality."[17] Don't lower your expectations based on what currently is. Instead, as Senge suggests, "Learn how to use the energy [the tension] generates to move reality more reliably toward [your] visions."[18]

Harnessing the magnetic force of vision is both a skill and a practice. And as with any skill, with practice you will increase your capacity to see from new vantage points. Be intentional about waking up and opening your eyes to the myriad futures available to you—any number of potential destinies are riding on your daily decisions. Don't be found asleep at the wheel! I think about what the great American poet W. S. Merwin lamented in his poem "The Estuary":

> we are asleep over charts at running windows
> we are asleep with compasses in our hands
> and at the bow of the stone boat
> the wave from the ends of the earth keeps breaking[19]

In the next chapter we will continue to awaken to the charts and compasses God has placed in our hearts and hands. You will continue practicing the art of vision casting as you set sail into the wide expanses of your future tomorrows. With a bird's-eye view of what's possible on the horizon, you will learn to leverage the creative tension that these potentialities generate. So even while you let your heart soar, you will learn to stay grounded by the internal bearings resident within your soul.

Cherish your visions and your dreams as they are the children of your soul, the blueprints of your ultimate achievements.

–NAPOLEON HILL

On the ocean of life let your mind be the ship and your heart be the compass.

—JAMES DAVID MANNING

・ ・ ・

CHAPTER NINE

Create Your Canvas

Create a vision of who you want to be—and
then live that picture as if it were already true.
–ARNOLD SCHWARZENEGGER

The Vision that you glorify in your mind, the
Ideal that you enthrone in your heart—this you
will build your life by, this you will become.
—JAMES ALLEN

WHAT DO OPRAH Winfrey, Kellan Lutz, Denny Hamlin, and Katy Perry all have in common? You guessed it. They all have made use of what has become popularly known as the vision board—as have many other famous celebrities, athletes, and high achievers. Most people believe that a vision board is a modern concept, but this isn't so. We find the same principle used by Jacob in the Book of Genesis. He understood the power of focus as if it were as universal as the law of gravity. Perhaps it was divine inspiration, but he discerned that like any other natural law, the principle was equally applicable whether you were a human being or a goat. He was dealt a set of circumstances and went about re-engineering them like a master craftsman.

After being repeatedly swindled by his father-in-law, Laban, who kept cheating him out of his share of flocks, Jacob used the gravitational pull of focus to turn things around. In a business negotiation with his uncle he agreed to continue to increase their venture's bottom line by overseeing the expansion of their herd. They agreed the single-color goats would belong to Laban, while the multicolor goats would belong to Jacob. Understanding the laws of focus, Jacob positioned multicolored branches in front of where the goats would be meditatively quenching their thirst multiple times a day. Here's how the story unfolds:

> So Jacob cut green branches from poplar, almond, and plane trees and peeled off some of the bark so that the branches had white stripes on them. He put the branches in front of the flocks at the watering places. When the animals came to drink, they also mated there, so the flocks mated in front of the branches. Then the young that were born were streaked, speckled, or spotted....When the stronger animals in the flock were mating, Jacob put the branches before their eyes so they would mate near the branches. But when the weaker animals mated, Jacob did not put the branches there. So the animals born from the weaker animals were Laban's, and those born from the stronger animals were Jacob's. In this way Jacob became very rich.
>
> —GENESIS 30:37–43, NCV

Now if the trajectory of an animal's genetic line was altered by what they saw, can you imagine the possibilities that await you once you discipline yourself to write a vision? There is power in what you fix your eyes upon—such as a vision board, which enables you to focus your view on a particular outcome you want to create. You could call it a viewfinder. What is the view you hope to find in your future? Remember, as we have already said, it works both ways: focus on what you don't want, and you'll only get more of it.

Whatever it is you focus on, good or bad, is what you will produce more of in your life. "What you focus on grows, what you think about expands, and what you dwell upon determines your destiny," writes business coach Robin Sharma. In other words, what you focus on becomes your reality. That is a powerful principle. What occupies your mind will ultimately determine the types of decisions you make day in and day out. And this is what makes a vision board such a wonderful tool for aiming your focus in the direction of your dreams.

A vision board is your canvas of future possibilities, a visual representation where images of what you want to see manifested in your life are gathered together so they can be reflected back to you on a consistent basis. It could be a bulletin board with pushpins, a poster board where you paste images with a glue stick, a decorative framed shadowbox where you collect photos or small items, or an old-fashioned picture ribbon board where you can easily insert and reinsert your favorite pictures.

The vehicle used to visually display your dreams and desires isn't as important as where you place it. As with Jacob's goats, it must be positioned somewhere you will repeatedly see it, wherever your watering hole is, be it your office wall, bathroom mirror, closet, or hallway—wherever it will catch your eye on a daily basis. The key is to prominently display that collection of images of how you want your life to look in the future. It's all about what you continually see with your eyes *and* your mind. Being able to actually see what your conscious mind desires to achieve will help your subconscious mind go to work on your behalf to make it possible. As we're told in Proverbs, as you think in your heart, so are you (Prov. 23:7). And as you've heard said, "You will see it when you believe it."

ONLY BELIEVE

The central message of the New Testament is rooted in the power of belief. In Romans we read that it is only "by believing in your heart that you are made right with God" (Rom. 10:10, NLT)—and in the Gospels we find the simple directive of Jesus to "only believe" (Mark 5:36; Luke 8:50). There is no other way to be made righteous, to enter God's kingdom, to inherit His great and precious promises, or to obtain eternal life. You must "only believe." It is another law akin to gravity—just as the gravitational pull of the earth keeps your feet on the ground, your faith-filled belief in God and His Word will pull you toward all that's possible in the kingdom. Jesus, as we read in the Gospel of John, is that very same Word in human form that "made his home among us" (John 1:14, NLT)—and today, by His Holy Spirit, continues to make His home in every believing heart.

Your life, therefore, follows your beliefs. If you want to change your life, you must change your beliefs about what is possible for you. "From your belief system you create your reality," writes author Jami Sell. This is how he explains it all works together with how you actually think:

> Your imagination takes the information you have pro-
> vided from your belief system and creates mental con-
> structs which you fuel by your strong emotional reactions

or passion. You provide information to your belief system by thinking. You think about something when you focus your attention onto it. You become what you behold. Since your reality is created by your beliefs you must change your beliefs to change your reality. Thinking changes your beliefs so to change your reality you must change your thinking. To change your thinking you must shift the focus of your attention to something new.[1]

This is exactly why visual images are so effective in helping you calibrate your beliefs about what's possible. Your subconscious mind, through what you are consciously perceiving, is much more likely to embrace a potential outcome your eyes can actually see. Your thoughts and imagination are like the ship's wheel, helping you control the direction you sail.

If you want to change your life, you must change your beliefs about what is possible for you.

You will want to harness the power of both your words *and* your thoughts. Thoughts without words are like a ship without a rudder, while words that aren't aligned with your beliefs are like a damaged or partially detached rudder. The ship's wheel is what controls the rudder, and they are both critical to effectively steering your ship and propelling you forward. That said, you must practice directing both your thoughts and your words. However, before you begin voicing your vision—which we will talk about in the next chapter—it is necessary to first focus your mind on visual images, something your eyes can behold.

Images hold more power in our minds than words do because our subconscious is wired to interpret what we see as real. (This is why our limited perceptions—which are really misperceptions—cause so many problems.) Therefore as you begin to set a new course forward, you'll need to establish a mental picture of what your desired destination actually looks like. You naturally did this when you envisioned how you wanted your life to look in the twelve areas we explored in the previous chapter. Now we are going to take those images you saw in your mind and bring them into the tangible present via your vision board.

BEGIN WITH THE END IN MIND

Plato may not have been the first to observe, "The beginning is the most important part of any work,"[2] but having said it, we attribute the observation to him. His student Aristotle followed the sentiment with this equally famous assertion: "Well begun is half done."[3] History continues to prove the validity of these statements. Any author, artist, inventor, or entrepreneur will tell you the heaviest lifting comes at the beginning of any endeavor—from constructing the outline of a book to drafting the blueprint for a building to crafting a strategic business plan, you must begin with the end in mind. Creating a life you love is no different. This is why God gave you the capacity to dream. The destination you dream of—or the journey you dream of taking to get there—is that end you are beginning with.

A *vision* is defined as "the ability to think about or plan the future with imagination" or a type of transcendent discernment, "a mental image projecting what the future will or could be."[4] It is something you can see in advance of the actual event. This is what I hoped to help you do in creating your life compass. You created "the substance" of the things you're hoping for (Heb. 11:1). With those ends in mind, you can begin scanning your environment or a pile of magazines or scouring the internet for images that represent them—and thereby giving them even more substance. Waking up and being alert to what you're looking for is a huge part of beginning well; it is beginning from a place of strength. You don't want to be caught unaware, as they say. And as Plato would agree, beginning from that alert place of strength will set you up for lasting success.

So the first task, now that you're awake to your desires, is simply to begin gathering pictures of how you want each of those twelve areas of your life to look—look for visual representations of the transformation you'd like to see in each area. Just by being awake and aware, you'll begin to notice images of what you're hoping to see—and often in unexpected places! You pass a bulletin board in the coffee shop; you see the cover of a pamphlet in the checkout line; you notice an ad in the newspaper. Could it be possible that the very things you are seeking have simply been beyond your view?

Begin training your mind to see what you're looking for. Find images that capture your attention, and grab hold of them; file them in a folder or deposit them in a gallon-sized zip-top bag. You can also flip through any magazine you come across and begin cutting out what you find there. For many, this will be a bigger project than you can sit down and do in one day, but today you can start gathering what you need to "grow" your vision board in the days and weeks ahead. Personally, I have found that identifying the images of what I truly want to see is the most labor-intensive process of creating a vision board.

HOW IT WORKS

Assembling your vision board is simply creating a blueprint or template of your envisioned future. It is the framework you will use to begin manifesting your dreams into reality. A vision board will help you not only focus on what you truly want but also eliminate whatever activities will distract you from achieving it. It will help you clarify and prioritize what is most important to you. This is what makes the vision board exercise so powerful. It helps focus your attention on what you want to the exclusion of everything else. A vision board helps your brain's information filtering system—known as the reticular activating system (RAS)—tune in to the opportunities that will move you closer to that desired reality. "Your RAS is responsible for filtering all the incoming information that your brain receives," writes author and expert Tristan Loo, "and it also acts as a receiver for information that is tagged as important."

> A simple way to conceptualize the RAS is to think of it like a radio. You are surrounded by radio waves from various stations and your portable radio can pick up those channels, but only one at a time. You have to tune your radio to a specific frequency of your favorite radio station in order to receive it properly. Your RAS is not much different in this regard.[5]

According to biologist Samuel Audifferen, "the human brain can store up to 100 trillion to 500 trillion bits of information."[6] Added to that massive amount of information, your RAS doesn't distinguish between what is a real event or an imagined one. A vision board allows you to exploit this phenomenon by enabling you to reprogram your RAS to seek out stimuli in your environment that resonate with your dreams.

> This selective attention filter makes you aware of daily things that can help you achieve your goal and it's your job to take action on those opportunities when they present themselves.[7]

Your subconscious mind responds to pictures and images that trigger an emotional reaction. Each picture on your vision board should therefore produce a positive emotional reaction when you look at it. Add words and phrases to the pictures that will increase the emotional draw to those pictured goals. Your vision board is only limited by how far your creativity and imagination can take you. Refuse to place limits on yourself as you construct your vision board! Keep it positive, motivating, and energized with God-inspired faith, founded in and backed by the promises in His Word, "for all the promises of God in Him are Yes, and in Him Amen, to the glory of God through us" (2 Cor. 1:20).

"I've learned that fear limits you and your vision," writes journalist Soledad O'Brien. "It serves as blinders to what may be just a few steps down the road for you."[8] Keep your radio tuned in to your kingdom potential—*all things* you can achieve and become through Christ (Phil. 4:13)!

PUTTING IT ALL TOGETHER

Once you've gathered all the images you want to use, determine the type of canvas you'd like to display them on. As we've said, you can use a bulletin board, poster board, ribbon board, or any large piece of cardboard. All you need is a surface large enough to assemble your pictures. Depending on the type of board you choose, you can tack or glue them or use double-sided tape. You may not have worked with glue and scissors since you were in grade school, so humor your inner child and enjoy the process!

The items you choose to include and how you choose to display them should resonate energetically with the emotions you want your board to elicit. How does that future state you're envisioning feel? For example, look for images that provoke a feeling of being empowered, loved, prosperous, peaceful, healthy, strong, respected, engaged, accomplished, and so on. These represent a state of being you're envisioning moving into—kind of like a geographical state where you hope to live one day. What does that look and feel like? What elements, colors, words, or arrangements might help stimulate that particular feeling? Arrange your pictures, words, and phrases on your board in a way that gives you a deep emotional connection to your vision. After you are satisfied with how the pictures are arranged, glue, tape, or tack your pictures in place.

Once your images are secured, add your own writing—a handwritten Bible verse, for example—or if you have a flair for drawing, accentuate your board with whatever artistic features will draw your attention and focus. Be creative and experiment with generating a positive energetic pull. You want your vision board not only to capture your dreamed-of destiny but also to inspire your imagination and spark a passionate, emotional charge within your soul. The vision board should charge you with renewed passion whenever you look at it.

Over time, as you move closer toward your desired future, some of the images may not make as much of an emotional impression as they once did. When you notice this, update your vision board with fresh images that still inspire you. Your vision board should always be a work in progress—a dynamic mirror of the deepest longings of your soul that changes as your dreams and desires change.[9] When it comes to creating your future, the energy you put into it is the energy you will get back out of it.

> Ninety-nine percent of all that is going to affect our tomorrows is being developed by humans using instruments and working in the ranges of reality that are non-humanly sensible.
>
> —BUCKMINSTER FULLER

> Write the vision, and make it plain on tablets, that he who reads it may run.
>
> —HABAKKUK 2:2, MEV

STEP FOUR

Dare to Do Something Great

The man without a purpose is like a ship without a rudder—a waif, a nothing, a no man. Have a purpose in life, and, having it, throw such strength of mind and muscle into your work as God has given you.
—THOMAS CARLYLE

Most assuredly, I say to you, he who believes in Me, the works that I do he will do also; and greater works than these he will do, because I go to My Father.
—JOHN 14:12

CHAPTER TEN

• • •

Voiceprint Your Vision

Throughout human history, our greatest leaders
and thinkers have used the power of words to
transform our emotions, to enlist us in their causes,
and to shape the course of destiny. Words can not
only create emotions, they create actions. And
from our actions flow the results of our lives.
—TONY ROBBINS

Never separate the life you live
from the words you speak.
—PAUL WELLSTONE

THERE'S A STORY told of a spy who, during the height of the Cold
War, sold US secrets to the Russians. Although an incriminating
phone conversation was recorded, the government was unable to
identify the spy. For five years he continued divulging sensitive
intelligence, but there was no way to associate his name with
the sound of his voice. While he was eventually caught because
of information provided by a Russian defector, he could have
been identified within seconds using a technology that was later

developed, commonly known as voiceprint technology. This technology was developed to capture certain voice patterns in a database and correlate them with an individual speaker. This algorithm created a "computer model of the individual's vocal characteristics," or a voiceprint. Journalist Ava Kofman writes, "The entire process—capturing a few spoken words, turning those words into a voiceprint, and comparing that representation to other 'voiceprints' already stored in the database—can happen almost instantaneously."[1]

Voice recognition software is now a part of our daily lives—from Alexa to Siri to our TV remote—and it is an identification mechanism used by the NSA along with fingerprints and face prints. Your voice is one of the most unique things about you, and it's so very important to learn how to leverage it. Your voice is powerful. It can be likened to a key only you can use to unlock doors of opportunity designed just for you or gain access to the powerful potential you carry—just like your smartphone, which opens up to you when you say "Hey, Siri." It's also the very thing the enemy wants to keep you from discovering. He wants you to suppress your voice—he wants to keep you from finding it and making it heard. This is why he works tirelessly to erode your confidence in speaking up or speaking out and most especially why he cleverly distracts you from praying.

Only you can speak to your future. No one can do it for you. Your tomorrow responds to your "Hello" alone. It is up to you to command your day and "pronounce something to be" (Job 22:28, voice)—that which you choose to do you must "decide and decree." When you declare a thing, "it will be established for you" (Job 22:28, amp). The key is being clear on what it is you're deciding upon declaring—and that's exactly why I've written this book.

That knowledge, along with knowing the truth about who you are in Christ, is what will keep you living long and prospering. (See Hosea 4:6, John 10:10, and 3 John 2.)

THE POWER OF YOUR WORDS

Your words carry such power they can change the environment—not just the atmosphere but also the physical landscape. Studies have shown that positive words deliberately spoken with mindful intention—such as declarative prayer—have positively impacted cities, water sources, and soil fertility.

In a famous study conducted by Japanese scientist Dr. Masaru Emoto, it was shown that water molecules change shape in response to spoken words. Hateful, critical words caused the water molecules to become distorted and ugly. Words of gratitude, love, and celebration caused the molecules to brighten into beautiful, symmetric designs.[2] That said, did you know that nearly 60 percent of the adult human body is water? In fact, the brain and heart are composed of 73 percent water, while the lungs are about 83 percent water! Like the frozen water crystals in Dr. Emoto's experiment, every thought, every emotion, every word causes your brain waves to take on specific "shapes." Your life will take on the positive or negative shape of the positive or negative words you speak as well as the positive and negative emotions you feel. Imagine the impact of giving thanks over your meal on the molecules in your food and drink! Your life and everything in it is affected by every word you speak.

"Words are the vibrations of nature," writes Dr. Emoto. "Therefore beautiful words create beautiful nature. Ugly words create ugly nature."[3] The Bible says it this way: "Death and life are in the power of the tongue" (Prov. 18:21). You might not feel as if you're seeing the effect of your words on your circumstances or in the environment around you, but they are always influencing change on every level. Words of gratitude like seeds will sprout more of what you are grateful for, while words of grumbling will sprout a thistle patch of more to grumble about. Be mindful of the words you speak, and use them to create the changes you want to see in your life, relationships, circumstances, and future.

FINDING YOUR UNIQUE VOICE

God has given you a unique voiceprint, just as He has a one-of-a-kind fingerprint. You are "fearfully and wonderfully made," writes David in Psalm 139:14. There are gifts He has bequeathed only to you (1 Pet. 4:10–11) and purposes only you can fulfill at this time in His-story.[4] Those unique gifts and callings have been seeded in your heart by Him as desires—lifelong dreams and visions that are unique to you. If you think back to your childhood, you can probably remember when you first discovered an interest or talent, or even certain experiences or encounters that you now know were forming you. What were these hinting to you about your unique voice and the unique sound you carry?

Remember that *voice* refers to one's "distinctive tone or style"—rooted in the Latin *vocare*, which means "to call" denoting an "invisible spirit or force that directs or suggests."[5] The same root, *vox*, is found in the words *invoke*, meaning to call upon; *evoke*, meaning to call forth; and *provoke*, meaning to incite—all words of activation.[6] Your voice, in other words, is an activating force. The sound of your voice transmits waves of energy—a unique frequency of "radiant energy that is transmitted by longitudinal pressure waves"[7]—that create a powerful energetic force. This force of energy permeates barriers, unlike light. In other words, light energy cannot break through a wall, whereas sound energy can. (Have you ever heard of the need to lightproof a wall?)

While you might not be able to shine light through a wall, you can speak light through it. Your distinctive tone is an invisible force that breaks through, calls forth, and directs transformative energy. You alone have the power to voiceprint your future. You can choose to speak life and light into it, or something else. You can decide to open the door of possibility or keep knocking on the door of frustration and futility. I imagine you are reading this because you want to step through to a better, brighter, higher place of influence and fulfillment—a place you know is possible simply because you've been able to imagine it. You've learned how to think like a visionary by practicing the art of possibility.

Your words have the power to change your direction, so use them wisely as you sail your ship of life toward the distant shore.

You mastered casting your vision in the light of your specific values in chapter 8 (your life compass) and crafting it in chapter 9 (your vision board)—and we've discussed how to put the power of visualization into practice. Now let's get down to the work of actually giving voice to your vision. A series of well-constructed vision statements that you can recall and repeat on a daily basis will add more fuel to the flame of the vision you've ignited. You've learned how to think and see as if your vision is a reality; now you will learn to speak as if it were so. When you are able to clearly articulate what it is you want to see come to pass, you will begin to voiceprint your future. Your desired reality will begin to take shape.

You are the author of the story you want your life to tell. It is up to you to give the hero you've imagined—that's you—a unique and powerful voice. Through a series of clearly articulated vision statements that you boldly declare over your future, you will begin to frame the structure of it, just like a shipbuilder frames a ship. You have already created the blueprint with your vision board; now you will erect a solid structure through the power of your words.

Your life is like raw clay that begs to be molded. Just as the formless cosmos was configured by the words God spoke when He declared, "Let there be light" (Gen. 1:3), it is incumbent upon you to speak light and form into your own life. In the New Testament we are told, "The universe was created by the word of God, so that what is seen was not made out of things that are visible" (Heb. 11:3, ESV). You can give form to your vision by the words you speak about what you would like to take shape in every area of your life. Speak "as if" just as you learned to write, think, and see "as if," using positive statements fashioned in the present tense. By using bold "I am" statements, for example, you begin to actively frame your future and mold yourself to fit the shape of the future reality you've envisioned. Don't underestimate the power of your words to steer you closer to the life of your dreams. The Book of James, when talking about the power of words, says, "Look also at ships: although they are so large and are driven by fierce winds, they are turned by a very small rudder wherever the pilot desires" (3:4). Your words have the power to change your direction, so use them wisely as you sail your ship of life toward the distant shore.

Look at your vision board and the images you've collected representing how you want your life to look in the twelve areas we discussed in chapter 8. Describe how your life would look and feel in the present moment based on what you see. Write a brief, present-tense statement about how life would currently be if it were how you envisioned it for each of the twelve areas. Display these statements near where you've displayed your vision board and wherever else you will see them often, boldly speaking them out whenever you do.

RUN TO WIN

World-class hurdlers have a unique approach to running their race. You will never hear a coach tell a sprinter, "Watch out for those hurdles." Instead, coaches train their runners to "attack" the hurdle head-on rather than slow down to carefully jump over the barrier. Charging the hurdle at full speed keeps runners from breaking their stride so they can maintain momentum. The same fearless drive that powers racers over hurdles can fuel your vision as well. Hurdles are to be expected in life—crises, unexpected changes, and disappointments are inevitable. The key to overcoming these difficulties is how you approach the barrier. Rather than letting fear, doubt, or indecision slow your momentum, confidently attacking the obstacle will carry you over the top.

For a runner, this strategy entails physical strength and endurance training. For a visionary, this requires you to find and strengthen your voice. A runner can see the finish line yet must use his legs to carry him there. You have a vision of a desired future and must use your voice to propel you in that direction. Your voice gives legs to your vision.

Your voice is like a muscle that you can strengthen. And like a muscle, it is strengthened by encountering resistance. You must discipline your words and align them with where you want to go regardless of the obstacles you encounter. You must speak with purpose just as a racer runs with purpose. If you've read any of my books—from *Commanding Your Morning* to *The 40 Day Soul Fast*—you'll know how passionate I am about the power of your words to change your life, your circumstances, and your destiny. And that happens primarily because of the power your words have to impact your own thoughts.

It is commonly believed that to change the way you speak, you must change the way you think. But just as putting a smile on your face changes your disposition, speaking positive words changes the neural pathways of your mind. It is impossible to speak words of gratitude while at the same time thinking resentful thoughts. In fact, speaking a blessing over someone else, or even over your meal, is perhaps more beneficial to the health of your own soul than anything else. So harness the power of your words to align your thoughts with the vision you have in your mind.

Your mind is predisposed to replaying the stories you've grown accustomed to telling yourself—repeating old scripts that are not serving your vision. To silence that inner saboteur, you'll need to rewrite the program. You'll have to reach beyond the thoughts you think on the surface of your conscious, wakeful mind to the bedrock of belief systems lying deep within. The most efficient way to reprogram your subconscious is to expose it to the sound of your voice telling a new story. This powerful practice will help silence the interior voices keeping you trapped in an old narrative.

> From the fruit of their lips people are filled with good
> things, and the work of their hands brings them reward.
> —PROVERBS 12:14, NIV

LEAN INTO FEAR

There's nothing that trips us up quite so effectively as our own fears, whether imagined or otherwise. Crafting a vision and seeing it through requires courage—and that courage will require you to find your voice and be willing to make it heard. "Courage," according to author Brené Brown, "originally meant 'To speak one's mind by telling all one's heart.'"[8] Fear is an invitation to speak. It is an invitation to look within and "tell all one's heart."

Fear itself is not the enemy, and if it were, it has absolutely no power other than what you give it. In fact, fear is simply a force you can use to either propel you forward or keep you tied down. You can actually choose to harness the energy fear generates for your own greater good. Comedian Bob Newhart puts it this way: "Fear is a friend who comes to visit me just before every show and he's been showing up for 52 years."[9] Fear is a powerful motivator and indicator that you are growing and building capacity by stretching yourself beyond your comfort zone. Fear compels you to suit up and show up—to put your stake in the ground, take a stand, and speak your truth.

When you feel anxious, speak to your heart by making positive affirmations; these are simply energy-charged confessions of faith. Don't neglect the power of your faith-filled words. The force your words carry redirects energy to undergird and sustain your vision while encouraging and strengthening your heart. Embrace the power of your voice to propel your vision forward. You should have twelve powerful present-tense statements capturing your vision of how things are in the future. You should have scripted a larger narrative of the story those "present" future circumstances tell and reframed any doubts or fears with truth-affirming, positive affirmations.

You not only will face opposition or resistance from within your own mind—conscious and subconscious—but will certainly encounter it from without: the circumstances that will oppose you, obstacles that stand in your way, or the opinions of others that can immobilize you. Not only can you use your voice to neutralize negative circumstances, clear away roadblocks, dispel darkness, and even calm storms (as we are told Jesus did in Mark 4:35–39), but you can speak life into opportunities you feel have withered and passed you by—you can speak light where there is confusion and chaos, and truth where deceptive forces conspire against your purpose.

Your vision acts as your map, your values as your compass, your thoughts and imagination as your ship's wheel, your words as your rudder, and your faith as your sails. These things work together to give your life direction and move it forward. Consider the story of young Jack Ma, who was born into a family that shared an income of seven dollars a month among six people. In 1972, at the tender age of six, he recalls hearing about President Nixon meeting with Chairman Mao Zedong, an event that solidified a trade relationship between China and the United States. He had no idea how he would use this information to create change in his country, but it was a seed that stirred his vision.[10]

As the events of his life unfolded, Ma turned out to be a subpar student—he was terrible at math and was denied admission twice to what he describes as "the worst university" in his home city. Rejection seemed to be the pen that wrote his success story, as he was turned down for admission by Harvard University ten times. He once applied for a job at Kentucky Fried Chicken, along with twenty-three other people, who were all hired; Ma was not.[11]

While visiting a friend in Seattle, Ma discovered the internet and began exploring the world of online commerce. He saw the potential for China to enter the online business market, believing it would facilitate opportunities for small enterprises there to do business with the rest of the world. This became his sole vision—and eventually, after many failures and rejections, he launched his company Alibaba. Alibaba went public in 2014 with the largest initial public offering ever, totaling $25 billion. Ma is currently among the world's top twenty wealthiest people.[12]

MAKE YOURSELF HEARD ABOVE THE NOISE

Part of finding your voice is actually making yourself heard! As important as it is to simply speak your vision out, you must also share it—not only with your family and friends but also with a wider network in your community and others in your field. The more you share your vision, the more power you give it, both by reinforcing it in your mind as well as garnering the support of others. This will also position you for greater success as a leader and influencer. As management consultant Marya Axner writes, "Learn how to use your vision to lead—to mobilize and inspire people so that others want to join you in making your vision a reality."[13] She continues:

> Talk to people about your vision as much as you can. Tell them what you are thinking. Give them your big picture of things. Then listen. See if other people are concerned about the same things you are concerned about....The more you talk to people and listen to them, the clearer your vision will become....Everyone doesn't necessarily have to agree with your vision for it to be a good one—but if people get animated and interested in talking with

you about your vision, that is a sign that you are onto something.[14]

Listening to how others respond and incorporating new ideas and suggestions will only make your vision stronger. Sharing your vision—or even components of it—will help refine it by bringing greater clarity, as well as growing it through the insights and ideas offered by others.

Is your vision bigger than you and what you can do on your own? There will be components of your vision that will require you to partner with others, that invite collaboration and harness the powerful synergy that is created when your vision and someone else's collide!

In the Bible, God shared His vision for humanity. He shared the positive expectation He had for His people (John 10:10). In speaking with His servant Jeremiah, He openly shared the vision He had for the future: "I know the thoughts that I think toward you...thoughts of peace, and not of evil, to give you an expected end" (Jer. 29:11, KJV). God also taught His people to "write the vision and make it plain" so others could run with it (Hab. 2:2).

SPEAK FOR A CHANGE

Vision casting—and crafting—is not a onetime event. It involves re-scripting your inner dialogue, re-landscaping the interior of your mind, and redirecting deeply rooted neural pathways. "Visioneering" involves the art and science of using the neuroplasticity of the brain (what we explored in chapter 6). It involves not only mindfully thinking for a change but also mindfully speaking for whole-life transformation.[15]

One of the forerunners in the field of positive psychology, along with Dale Carnegie and Norman Vincent Peale, was Wilferd Arlan Peterson. He understood the scope of neuroplasticity to frame the human experience and the power each of us has to shape our reality:

> As a single footstep will not make a path on the earth, so a single thought will not make a pathway in the mind. To make a deep physical path, we walk again and again. To make a deep mental path, we must think over and over the kind of thoughts we wish to dominate our lives.[16]

Your life is governed by your thoughts—and the best way to direct your thoughts is to direct your words. You must tell your mind what to think.[17] How you think and speak is a matter of habit. Changing a habit or lifestyle you've become accustomed to is difficult—it takes conviction, courage, and willpower applied over time to truly change the course of your life.

You've crafted a clear and compelling vision based on your core values. You've learned to think like a visionary and use the power of a vision board and the practice of visualization to move you closer to that vision every day. You've drafted powerful vision statements you can repeat and share. You've learned how to use the force of your words to magnetize your vision, and the power of your voice to safeguard and amplify it. Most importantly you've learned the impact that sharing your vision can have on your own life and the world around you.

When you are able to clearly articulate what it is you want to see come to pass, you will begin to voiceprint your future. Harness the power of your words to align your thoughts with the vision of the future you have in mind—undergirded by the force of your positive expectation. See the appendix for some powerful Bible-based declarations and prayers to help you start using the power of words.

> I tell you the truth, you can say to this mountain, "May you be lifted up and thrown into the sea," and it will happen. But you must really believe it will happen and have no doubt in your heart.
>
> —MARK 11:23, NLT

> Place these words on your hearts. Get them deep inside you. Tie them on your hands and foreheads as a reminder....Talk about them wherever you are, sitting at home or walking in the street; talk about them from the time you get up in the morning until you fall into bed at night.
>
> —DEUTERONOMY 11:18–19, THE MESSAGE

♦ ♦ ♦

CHAPTER ELEVEN

Ignite Your Divine Genius

I am convinced all of humanity is born with
more gifts than we know. Most are born
geniuses and just get de-geniused rapidly.
—Buckminster Fuller

In the smallest slices of time we meet
our biggest opportunities to become
what we are capable of becoming.
—Robert Cooper

As I've studied the lives of history-making geniuses, I've come
to discover some common threads. We've already talked about
Leonardo da Vinci's famed *sapere vedere*—"knowing how to see"—
but there are other methods of counteracting the de-geniusing that
Fuller speaks of in the quote above. In this chapter I want to help
you activate a few simple, yet powerful, strategies that will ignite
your genius and add rocket fuel to your vision.

In my years of working with people from all around the world
and from all walks of life, I have been most troubled by how
many are unaware of or simply ignore their own divine genius.

This observation has fueled my mission to empower people to discover their highest purpose and maximize their greatest potential. This is the driving force behind all my books—from my series of prayer books[1] to *Commanding Your Morning* to *PUSH* to *Proclaim* to *History Maker*. Even the Soul Series offers different aspects of how to take back your personal power once and for all.[2] Nothing saddens and frustrates me more than seeing people squander their potential. That said, if there is something that deeply saddens or frustrates you, it could be a clue to your own higher purpose and calling. As we talked about in chapter 4, where your core desires, values, and causes intersect is where you'll find the controlling idea of your life purpose.

If you want to serve, serve on purpose. If you want to give, give on purpose. If you want to lead, lead on purpose. Learn how to leverage the wealth of your own divine genius.

YOUR GENIUS AND YOUR DREAM

I'm reminded of the story of the history-making dreamer Joseph, the son, grandson, and great-grandson of the great patriarchs of faith—Jacob, Isaac, and Abraham. When "Joseph the Dreamer"[3] went to work for Potiphar as a field hand on his estate, it was not long before he was running the place. Was he still a servant? Yes. Potiphar was in charge—no question about it—but Potiphar was an army general, not a farmer or an estate manager. He was good at winning battles, not at growing and storing crops, getting the best deal for his surplus in the marketplace, or managing the day-to-day affairs of his home. If Joseph had only done the things Potiphar had asked him to do, Potiphar's estate would have been no better than it was before. But under Joseph, his assets grew as never before.

Why? Because Joseph understood how to tap into his divine genius to best serve his master. He had a gift for learning and administration. He was able to incorporate lessons from his father about managing a large estate and improve upon the systems and practices Potiphar already had in place. He studied the surrounding enterprises to glean their best practices and turned Potiphar's holdings into an increasingly prosperous venture. Joseph helped Potiphar get what he wanted, but not by simply doing what Potiphar thought he needed Joseph to do. Joseph took the initiative to apply his genius to Potiphar's affairs, and when he did, Potiphar delegated to him executive decision-making authority because he "saw that the LORD was with [Joseph] and that the LORD made all he did to prosper in his hand" (Gen. 39:3).

Sometimes you need to see beyond what people ask you to do, because most people don't know what it is want, let alone how to get it. They stumble through, looking for some evanescent version of success, as if they were wandering around in a storm hoping to get hit by lightning. They are looking for their big break, waiting for their ship to come in, chasing the next wrung up the ladder, without giving much thought to pursuing a legacy-driven destiny. It's in navigating beyond the conflicting waves of other people's needs and opinions that you will discover the higher ground of true success, prosperity, and fulfillment.

You must take ownership of your own divine destiny and be strategic about bringing it to pass. It is up to you to understand, initiate, and doggedly pursue your greater potential. The day will come when you'll be required to give an answer for the choices you've made, when you'll have to look into the reflection of that "hope and future" God imagined for you and acknowledge how you measured up. At that time, when He shows you how He sees your identity in Christ and the authority He's given you in His name—the world's "hope of glory" (Col. 1:27)—will you have fallen short? I believe that is why you're reading this book. You are seeking to be that "good and faithful servant" (Matt. 25:21–23).

PUTTING YOUR GENIUS TO WORK

So how can you begin to tap into the power of your unique genius? Gina Rudan, author of *Practical Genius*, defines *genius* as the intersection of "your unique strengths, skills, expertise, passions, creativity, and values."[4] On the ends of that spectrum of characteristics, we find strengths and values. If we examine the intersection of values and strengths, with values on the horizontal axis and strengths on the vertical axis, it would create a chart that looks something like this:

Let's take a look at each of these quadrants.

Low value/low strength (lower left)

These are the things that are not very important and you are not so good at doing. They are the common time traps that keep you from accomplishing your major goals, and they are quite literally a complete waste of your time. If something in this area needs to be done, delegate it.

High value/low strength (lower right)

These things are important, but you're not so good at them. These could be activities—such as accounting, landscaping, or even cleaning your house—that someone else could probably do more efficiently or cost effectively. While you can do these things because they are important, it is better to delegate them since you are not good at them.

Low value/high strength (upper left)

These are things that you are good at doing but don't yield a high return on your time investment—neither do they give you much satisfaction or joy. You may do them well, but they may leave you feeling exhausted or distract you from doing higher-value activities. These things can be delegated to others as needed.

High value/high strength (upper right)

This is the genius zone. These are the things you excel at doing that move you forward in a significant way—things that no one else can do better than you and leave you feeling energized. This is where your creativity pushes its limits and you feel the weight of your contribution making a difference. You are giving that talk to an auditorium full of people, writing that book, creating those videos, doing your podcast, leading an exercise for the business or organization that has hired you to consult with it—the primary activities your career or company is built upon.

So aside from eliminating the low-value/low-strength (time-wasting) and perhaps even those low-value/high-strength activities (just because you do something well doesn't mean you—or anyone—should do it), you are left with the option of delegating the high-value/low-strength activities. That said, you may not feel you're currently in a position to delegate the high-value/low-strength activities to someone else, yet you can still delegate—or relegate—them to specific, limited times in your day. Without getting too much into time-management techniques, you can batch similar activities together so it's easier to remain focused on your genius-zone activities for the majority of your time.

In one of his recent podcast riffs, author and entrepreneur Jonathan Fields asked these questions:

> What if you blew up your schedule and rebuilt it around your ability to birth genius? What if you started with a blank, white schedule, then added in four to five hours a day in fluid bursts where you dropped into uninterrupted, hyper-focused maker mode? What if then, and only then, you added back in a smattering of "manager mode" items...but only what could fit into a designated two- to three-hour window every day? And what if you kept this schedule for a week, or a month, or a season?[5]

This is not so different from the illustration offered years ago by Stephen R. Covey when he compared time management to filling a jar with sand and rocks. In one instance, he first inserted the sand followed by smaller rocks so that the biggest rocks wouldn't fit. Conversely, when he first inserted the biggest rocks, representing the highest-value items, followed by the smaller rocks, and finally the sand of minutia, everything fit (even the minutia!).[6]

It's one thing to have priorities, but it's quite another to prioritize the time necessary to actually achieve them. By intentionally allocating blocks of time that keep you in that quadrant where you operate from your genius—where your highest strengths and values intersect—you accelerate your success and impact.

MAXIMIZE YOUR GENIUS ZONE

When you are fully operating in your divinely given genius zone, you could say that you have found your *flow*—"the mental state in which a person performing an activity is fully immersed in a feeling of energized focus, full involvement, and enjoyment in the process of the activity."[7] This is also commonly known as "being in the zone" and something you more often hear in relation to athletic performance. However, according to psychologist Mihály Csíkszentmihályi, who popularized the term *flow* in the early 1990s, it is simply an "optimal state of consciousness where we feel our best and perform our best." He explains, "Your whole being is involved, and you're using your skills to the utmost."[8]

This also means that what you're doing is just challenging enough to stretch you but not so challenging that it causes stress. The key is finding that balance and maintaining it—and therefore your energized focus—as much as possible. If you're going to reap the harvest of the vision you've been planting, you must learn to expertly cultivate both your energy and your time.

In his book *The Power of When*, Michael Breus argues that every person's biology is predisposed to being most productive at certain times of day. He outlines four chronotypes that explain how an individual is naturally inclined to function throughout the day and night. These four types are depicted by Dr. Breus as the wolf, the bear, the lion, and the dolphin. A wolf-type, for example, is more nocturnal, while a lion-type is the morning-oriented early riser. The bear-type enjoys a good nap, while the dolphin-type has less of a sleep drive altogether.[9] Knowing your chronotype can help you understand when the best time of day (or night) is for you to operate in your genius zone and find that optimum flow state. Dr. Breus offers a free online quiz that will quickly enable you to discover your own chronotype.[10]

Another recently published book, *When: The Scientific Secrets of Perfect Timing* by Daniel Pink, also explores when an individual's optimal time of day is for various activities. He offers a more universal view of when certain types of tasks should be undertaken. For example, Pink indicates that morning is a good time for certain activities, while certain activities should be avoided during the early to midafternoon trough because of impaired judgment. Pink does, however, concur that chronotypes do have an effect.[11] Generally human performance experts agree that those who make the most of their mornings position themselves for greater productivity and success.[12] And the Bible has multiple examples of people rising early in the morning to accomplish important tasks. After Jacob dreamed of the ladder, he "rose early in the morning" to set up the stone pillar and make his vow (Gen. 28:18). When it was time to fight the battle of Jericho, "Joshua rose early in the morning" (Josh. 6:12). And when he was going out to the battlefield where the children of Israel were facing the Philistines, including Goliath, "David rose early in the morning" (1 Sam. 17:20).

If you're going to reap the harvest of the vision you've been planting, you must learn to expertly cultivate both your energy and your time.

Suffice it to say, timing could very well be everything. So not only can you expand your genius zone by understanding *what* is most valuable for you to focus on, but you can turbocharge it by understanding *when* is most valuable for you. Success in any endeavor is about managing your resources—and your greatest resources are your time and energy. When you are able to clarify those few things worthy of your undivided attention, and when best to pursue them, you will be light years ahead of most everyone else.

EMBRACE YOUR INNER GENIUS

For you to maximize your impact, you need to maximize the time you spend doing what you are best at and those things that will move you farther across the sea toward your ultimate goals. However, walking in your divinely given genius isn't all about what you do when; it's also a state of mind. It is connecting to your true power source—God (Phil. 2:13).

Your state of mind is rooted in how you see yourself—who you believe yourself to be, or your identity. It is determined by the standards you've set for yourself based on your self-worth and your confidence in God, who makes all things possible (Matt. 19:26). You may have believed the narratives other people have spoken over your character, capabilities, or worth—or you may have eroded your self-confidence by repeatedly breaking the promises or agreements you've made with yourself. Either other people or your own psyche has caused you not to fully trust yourself. Each of these external and internal scripts will lead to incongruences and insecurities when it comes to what you believe about who you are.

"You'll never exceed in your life what you think you're worth," explained business and leadership expert Ed Mylett in a recent interview with Shawn Stevenson. "Your identity is your self-worth, what you believe you deserve."[13] He went on to describe it this way:

Self-worth and identity are like a thermostat. It sits on the wall of your life, it sets the entire temperature for your life. So you have a spiritual thermostat, a financial, a business, a physical one, a wellness one. So if that thermostat is set at let's say financially at eighty degrees, it's set at eighty degrees, no matter what you do, you've already experienced it. If you start to heat your life up, you start having abundance come into it and you're doing activities that are better but you haven't changed your identity, you will find a way to cool your life right back down to where your identity is eventually.[14]

The key, according to Mylett, is to change the thermostat level of what you think you're worth: "You could be in the best business model with the best opportunity, the best products, the best everything, and you will not exceed eighty degrees of identity if that's the identity in your life."[15]

Stevenson pointed out that "the number one driving force of the human psyche is to stay congruent with the ideas we carry of ourselves." In his response, Mylett said:

You will do everything in the world to become congruent with your identity, so you'd better put a governor on it....I can do all the tactics, all the strategies, all the things you teach me, but if my identity is still way down here, that's the result I'm going to produce....What we get in our life is our standards. Habits and rituals deliver us on whatever standard we set which is governed by our identity.[16]

Your identity must be founded on truth. And the truth is that because of Jesus Christ you are a child of God (Rom. 8:16), a new creation (2 Cor. 5:17), and an overcomer (1 John 5:4). You are blessed (Eph. 1:3), chosen (1 Pet. 2:9), complete (Col. 2:10), forgiven (Eph. 1:7), loved (Jer. 31:3), valuable (Luke 12:7), and victorious (1 Cor. 15:57). You are no longer a slave to fear (Rom. 8:15) or a slave to sin (Rom. 6:5–7). You are the temple of the living God (2 Cor. 6:16).

So before we start talking about strategies and tactics—the structures, habits, and routines you'll need to put in place to move you forward day in and day out—you must upgrade your perception of your identity. You must keep the agreements you make with yourself—no matter how small. Make it a daily practice to build upon those agreements. Set the alarm a little earlier and get out of bed when you intended to; set a goal to read ten pages of a book every night and do it; go on that daily walk during your lunch break you keep meaning to; do what you know you should do but often neglect. As Jim Rohn is remembered for saying, "The things that are easy to do are also easy *not* to do. That's the difference between success and failure."[17]

You can begin to up the thermostat on your life first thing in the morning. "How you start the day upgrades or downgrades your whole day," states neuroscientist Robert Cooper.[18] There has indeed been a great deal published regarding the power of a morning routine. Probably second to having a clear and compelling vision, successful people have a regular morning routine that goes beyond grabbing a cup of coffee on the way out the door. Set yourself up—that is your state of mind—for making the most of your divine genius by practicing a spirit-, soul-, and body-rejuvenating morning routine. It is a *practice* that you can build and improve upon. Not only will this help you make the most of your day, but it will also force you to be more diligent with your evenings. And as you will have learned from reading *Commanding Your Morning*, making the most of your day begins before it ever dawns.

This is where the *Hello, Tomorrow!* rubber really meets the road! It is in bookending your day with your vision firmly in mind—practicing those visualization techniques and routinely speaking over your life—that your sails of faith will catch the wind of passion, moving you ever closer to the shore of your destiny.

> It is in your moments of decision that your destiny is shaped.
>
> —TONY ROBBINS

> I discovered I always have choices, and sometimes it's only a choice of attitude.
>
> —JUDITH M. KNOWLTON

◆ ◆ ◆

CHAPTER TWELVE

Discover Your New Frontier

And he has given you a destiny—*something to do in this life, something only you can do.* Before you were born, God wired you with certain ambitions, desires, and drives to play a particular role in history—one that only you can play.
—RICK WARREN

Your eyes saw my substance, being yet unformed. And in Your book they all were written, the days fashioned for me, when as yet there were none of them.
—PSALM 139:16

ON JULY 15, 1960, John F. Kennedy addressed a crowd of fifty thousand people who had gathered at the Memorial Coliseum in Los Angeles to hear his response to being nominated for president. It was during a difficult time in history when the United States was launching into the Cold War while nearby Cuba had just installed a Communist regime. In the face of uncertainty and threat, Kennedy boldly delivered a speech in which he stated, "We stand today on the edge of a New Frontier...the frontier of unknown opportunities and perils, the frontier of unfilled hopes and unfilled threats. . . . The New Frontier of which I speak is not a set of promises. It is a set of challenges."[1]

Kennedy understood that wherever there are new frontiers, there are new challenges. As much as a new frontier brings with it the promise of new opportunities, it also brings uncertainty. Kennedy's acceptance speech is worth considering today—not only in regard to the state of our nation sixty years later but as it relates to the current state of our minds. In light of current events and what I call "cultural confidence" (not unlike "consumer confidence," which is "the degree of optimism about the state of the economy"[2]), consider the words Kennedy delivered in his acceptance speech that day:

> I believe that the times require imagination and courage and perseverance. I'm asking each of you to be pioneers towards that New Frontier. My call is to the young in heart, regardless of age—to the stout in spirit, regardless of Party, to all who respond to the scriptural call: "Be strong and of a good courage; be not afraid, neither be dismayed." For courage, not complacency, is our need today; leadership, not salesmanship. And the only valid test of leadership is the ability to lead, and lead vigorously.[3]

In my book *History Maker* I challenge readers to rise up and take their place in leading change. I offer strategies for creating the inner healing of hearts and minds so neighborhoods, workplaces, and nations can be healed. I think of the recently elected prime minister of Ethiopia, who has done more to cultivate peace and inspire hope throughout his nation than previous leaders have done in decades—creating an environment that inspires confidence, where measurable economic changes are now rippling throughout the region. Kennedy spoke about governing in such a way that "we witness not only new breakthroughs…but also…mastery of the sky…the far side of space, and the inside of men's minds." He continued:

> That is the question of the New Frontier. That is the choice our nation must make…between the public interest and private comfort, between national greatness and national decline, between the fresh air of progress and the stale, dank atmosphere of "normalcy," between dedication and mediocrity.…A whole world looks to see what we shall do.…Recall with me the words of Isaiah that, "They who wait upon the Lord shall renew their strength; they shall mount up with wings as eagles; they shall run and not be weary." As we face the coming great challenge, we too, shall wait upon the Lord, and ask that He renew our strength. Then shall we be equal to the test. Then we shall not be weary. Then we shall prevail.[4]

MEETING THE PERSON YOU'RE DESTINED TO BE

Every day you are given an opportunity to close the gap between who you're dreaming of becoming and what you're destined to do—in other words, engaging in that capacity-building process that will take you from what you're capable of now to your greater potential. There is the upgraded version of you and your life that hopefully by now you were able to imagine, articulate, and get very specific about as you developed your life compass, constructed your vision board, and crafted the statements you can now declare and share. You've created that dynamic tension between what is and what could be that will energize your focus and pull you forward—like light that attracts a moth, or the pull of attraction of a magnet. The clearer you are about what is attracting you—or is *most* attractive—about that other version of you, the stronger the pull will be.

Wherever you are in life, never stop pursuing that next version of you. Never stop growing and expanding your capacity to have greater influence in the lives of those around you and those you may never meet, in this generation as well as the next. No matter what your faith is, you are most likely aware that history is being made in one way or another by the life you live—regardless of what you choose to do or don't do, whether you rise to your potential or not, you will be required to give an accounting. When you do, will you be shown an alternative version of yourself that you could have been—the influential, legacy-leaving, history-making version that God destined you to be? Will you recognize that person? Will you be total strangers? Or will you meet your twin?

I've always tried to imagine the version of myself I will meet when God introduces me to the person He'd hoped I'd become, the version that walks in the fullness of the identity and authority He called me up to in Christ. There is so much untapped potential we carry—especially those of us who have inherited "the promises that enable [us] to share his divine nature" (2 Pet. 1:4, NLT). "The comfortable road will never lead you to the person you were destined to be ever in your life," shares performance expert Ed Mylett. "If you don't become obsessed with chasing that person, you end up never meeting him." This is what fuels him to make the choices he does every single day: "Every decision I make, the things I go through in my life, whether I'm going to go to the gym, whether I'm going to make a phone call, how I'm going to eat, does it get me close to that guy?"[5] His desire to meet that destiny-defined person is greater than his desire to be comfortable. The point is, *your new frontier lies just beyond your comfort zone.*

If you are too comfortable where you are right now in your life, you are probably not engaged in that chase. You are not running to win the race set before you (1 Cor. 9:24). Instead, you are sitting on the sideline of your own life, sipping lemonade in the shade. Only when you are in hot pursuit of the best version of yourself are you making good on the promise God created you to share with your life. You carry the seeds of solutions, the missing pieces of a puzzle, and the answers to someone's prayer simply by faithfully stewarding the dreams and desires God has deposited in your heart. That vision you carry is the foundation of what I call your "personal brand"—it's the unique statement you're here to make, the promise you stand for, the signature you will leave with the impressions you make.

So what will that mark of distinction be that is left in the wake of your daily life, the stamp of today that will mark your tomorrow? I think of a master craftsman's unique stamp used to "brand" items from art to furniture to jewelry to leather goods from the days of medieval European guilds—these were originally referred to as maker's marks. Each good the craftsman deemed worthy was marked with a distinctive "seal of approval." This was how a particular brand became known and trusted in the early marketplaces of Europe. You are the master craftsman of your life, so what is that distinctive mark people will know you by? Personal branding is powerful—both as a strategy to magnify your influence and as a mechanism to hold you accountable to that distinctive person you are destined to be.[6]

DON'T BECOME YOUR OWN BEST IMPERSONATOR

In his book *Turning Pro*, Steven Pressfield talks about the fact that each of us has a great work to accomplish on the earth, whether it's as a novelist, a car mechanic, a politician, or whatever. Each of us has a contribution to make to the world in a very specific way that bubbles up out of our very being. The trouble is, rather than actually living that life, most of us settle for something close to that life or at best parallel to it—like taking the frontage road that runs alongside the highway; it appears as if it's taking you where you want to go but doesn't. We allow ourselves to live in the shadow of what we were meant to accomplish without actually achieving it. We give in to the fear of stepping out toward that new frontier and settle instead for something that feels closer to home but is much, much less meaningful to the world around us—*and to us.*

At best, that means a person who is a writer at his or her core might accept the freewheeling life of a truck driver instead, exploring the highways and byways of the open road rather than exploring the inner roads of his or her soul as the person was actually created to do. At worst, it means we let addictions—drugs, alcohol, video games, making money, the internet, pleasing others, and so forth (the more socially acceptable the addiction, the more insidious it is)—numb the effects of living without creating. We accept life in the shadows rather than stepping out into the light of where we were really meant to live.

The way of the addict is to live counterfeit to our true calling—similar but not the same—a silhouette of our authentic, divine selves; just a step or two inside of our comfort zone away from what we are actually meant to do. We allow our addictions to anesthetize the pain of living without true fulfillment.

The way of "the pro," as Pressfield describes it, is to step outside of our comfort zone and actually do the work of creating our contribution to the rest of the world. "Turning pro," according to Pressfield, is simply doing the work we were created to do regardless of its initial success or impact. The amateur plays at it but never buckles down to *do the work* for a thousand different, and usually fairly reasonable, reasons. Only the professionals—who do the work their souls call them to do—really live the life that is truly life, while the amateur never quite steps out from the shadows of living life as an impersonator.[7]

Don't imitate who it is you know you're capable of becoming; boldly step out into the fullness of it. Become—as in "come into being"—and fully identify with that writer, thought leader, advocate, entrepreneur, artist, or professional whatever it is. The decision is yours to identify with the addict or the artist—the poser or the professional—the time clock puncher or the self-starting entrepreneur. You have the divine agency to choose.

UNDERTAKE A NEW VENTURE

Personally, I have a passion for entrepreneurialism. I can identify with those who proclaim themselves to be "serial entrepreneurs" (which makes me want to ask, "What do you proclaim yourself to be?"). Unlike how most people define an entrepreneur (i.e. anyone who starts a business), the word is rooted in the old French *entreprendre*, meaning "to undertake"[8]—so a more accurate definition would be "someone who undertakes a venture." Dictionaries commonly define it as something along the lines of "a person who starts a business and is willing to risk loss in order to make money," or "one who organizes, manages, and assumes the risks of a business or enterprise."[9] This echoes the more conventional use of the word I described.

However, what I would like to emphasize is that a true entrepreneur is not just someone with the gumption to start a business but rather someone with an idea whose time has come. As Brett Nelson wrote in *Forbes* magazine, "Entrepreneurs, in the purest sense, are those who identify a need—any need—and fill it. It's a primordial urge, independent of product, service, industry or market....This is the true essence of entrepreneurship: Define, invest, build, repeat."[10] According to Russell Sobel,

> An entrepreneur is an agent of change. Entrepreneurship is the process of discovering new ways of combining resources....An entrepreneur who takes the resources necessary to produce a pair of jeans that can be sold for thirty dollars and instead turns them into a denim backpack that sells for fifty dollars will earn a profit by increasing the value those resources create.[11]

One of my favorite definitions is the one used by Harvard Business School professor Howard Stevenson: "Entrepreneurship is the pursuit of opportunity without regard to resources currently controlled."[12] In other words, entrepreneurship is not about having a business or certain set of skills; it's about having an idea that you can turn into a venture that meets a need—as well as the perseverance to pursue it regardless of what you do or don't have, what others say, or what conventional wisdom tells you is or isn't possible.

An entrepreneur is a person willing to take on the improbable and unreasonable. Such entrepreneurs are not hindered by lack of capital or resources because their main currencies of trade are brainpower and the grit to see their dreams through to realization. They don't throw money at ideas; they attack ideas with all they are worth and figure out solutions no one else has seen in the same light. They see deficits in the market others have yet to exploit, develop a venture to fill those deficits, and then generate revenue by meeting perceived needs. What they create is not exploitation but win-win outcomes. They fill a need so their customers can be more successful, happy, healthy, or fulfilled.

There is an old saying that "necessity is the mother of invention." What that means is where there is a need, there is an opportunity to innovate a solution. However, the need is more father than mother; it may provide the seed of the idea, but it is imagination that germinates that seed and brings it to fruition. Therefore, I like to say that imagination is the true mother of invention. We must never forget that our minds—our imaginations—are always our greatest assets. As Napoleon Hill famously put it, "Whatever your mind can conceive and believe, it can achieve."[13] Whatever you focus your mind on will prosper. Are you going to invest your focus on things such as television or social media, or on creating something that makes the world we're actually living in a better place?

TAKE FIRM HOLD OF YOUR TOMORROW

"One good mechanism beats a hundred good plans," states neuroscientist Robert Cooper. "There is a world of difference between imagining a fulfilling life and actually living it."[14] So what are those mechanisms that will enable you to live the life you've imagined? One of those mechanisms as we've learned has to do with the types of questions you ask. Again, the questions you ask determine your thoughts and therefore your actions. But as much as you determine to think "new frontier thoughts" and take pioneering actions, your brain is actually wired to keep you homebound.

There is a part of your neurobiology called the *amygdala* that "is the reason we are afraid of things outside our control. It also controls the way we react to certain stimuli."[15] Your amygdala relentlessly urges you to "favor the familiar and routine" because it is engineered to desire control and safety. "The amygdala's instincts...tend to spill over into every aspect of life and promote a perpetual reluctance to embrace anything that involves risk, change, or growth," explains Dr. Cooper.[16] In other words, it wants you to be what you've always been and stay just the way you are. "Unless you choose to consciously override this brain tendency, you're consigned to repeating the past," he warns.[17] This may sound disheartening to those gearing up to launch out into the big blue yonder of their future, but there are some specific things you can do to move from the life you've imagined into the life you actually live.

"There's a simple mechanism that overcomes our natural resistance to growth or change and helps us be our best," suggests Cooper. "All that is required is to regularly ask these two questions: 1. What's the most exceptional thing you've done this week [or today]? 2. What's the most exceptional thing you'll do next week [or tomorrow]?"[18] By *exceptional* he means those things that stood out or caused you to go against the crowd, actions you took that made a real difference in the lives of others or that made you proud.

> This mechanism stimulates a simple yet significant shift in the way we look at ourselves. It gets past good intentions and proclamations. It prompts a deeper way of recognizing the times you could reach for the exceptional....It steadily raises your sights about what you are actually capable of bringing and doing and becoming....This heightens curiosity about the possibilities for taking new actions. You'll be more likely to find yourself actively

seeking ways to give the world more of your best instead of just hoping for opportunities to arise.[19]

It is only by consistent, intentional effort that you are able to override the don't-grow-or-change instincts of your brain. It takes daily action—employing simple mechanisms that yield truly transformational results. "Although we may dream about our future in splendid images, we must live our lives in practical everyday actions, one after another," affirms Cooper.[20] This is "where our spirit wakes up and rises...where we break old habits and start shaping a far better future."[21]

It is through your daily actions that you will awaken to your hidden capacities. And it is your repeated behaviors that drive your attitudes, your daily disposition that determines what you choose to focus on—not the other way around. If you want to feel happy, then smile; if you want to feel brave, then stand taller; if you want to feel generous, then give something away. You must first do something before you feel something.[22]

It is time to step to the helm of your ship with the sails of faith billowing out as they catch the wind of passion.

Likewise, vision requires strategy for it to come to pass. "Vision without action is a dream," writes futurist Joel Barker. On the other hand, "action without vision is simply passing the time," he adds.[23] Don't get caught dreamily passing the time, but actively and strategically pursue your dream. What do you need to do today to take you where you want to be tomorrow? Create a series of action steps undergirded by the practices and mechanisms you've learned here. Stay open to and aware of the people and opportunities that present themselves, and learn to make the most of how you harness your time and genius. Most importantly, take control of those internal scripts. Remember, the Bible tells us that as you think, so are you (Prov. 23:7). It also lets us know that we can take control of our thoughts, "bringing every thought into captivity to the obedience of Christ" (2 Cor. 10:5). The journey to your dreamed-of frontier is more than anything else determined by what you believe is possible for you—tell yourself a new story about the hero you choose to be. Your vision is what allows you to put your greatness on display because it raises the bar on what you believe is possible. And we know that "all things are possible to him who believes" (Mark 9:23).

Position yourself today to make the most of tomorrow's promise. Imagine who you can become in the days, months, and years ahead—who is that future version that beckons to you? Pick up the line when your future self calls and says "Hello!" Your future is calling, demanding your response. You might as well answer with vision in hand. Don't let the phone keep ringing!

Take action. In fact, take the initiative to ignite your divine genius by calling out to that person you know you can be, doing the things you have been uniquely wired to do, and accomplishing the goals you have been gifted to achieve. Whether your goals are personal, spiritual, relational, financial, professional, or industry-specific, it is time to set sail. It is time to step to the helm of your ship with the sails of faith billowing out as they catch the wind of passion. It is time to steer your ship with the wheel of your thoughts and imagination and the rudder of your words, using the map of vision, the compass of values, and the north star of desired direction. It is time to expertly guide your vessel toward the distant shore of destiny, unencumbered by the anchor of fear or the barnacles of negative emotions on the hull of your mind. When you look back to who you are today and see the compass you created and the map you laid out, your future self will respond with "Land ho!" and a resounding "Thank you, captain" from the approaching shore of your dreamed-of destination. "The New Frontier is here whether we seek it or not," Kennedy said.[24] It's entirely up to you whether you step into it.

> Beyond that frontier are uncharted areas of science and space, unsolved problems of peace and war, unconquered problems of ignorance and prejudice, unanswered questions of poverty and surplus. It would be easier to shrink from that new frontier, to look to the safe mediocrity of the past, to be lulled by good intentions and high rhetoric.
> —JOHN F. KENNEDY

> With God all things are possible.
> —MATTHEW 19:26

EPILOGUE

◆ ◆ ◆

PRAYERFULLY, BY NOW you have grasped the transformational power of vision—that mental image of future potentialities that connects you to God's plan for your life (Jer. 29:11). Vision does not look back but looks ahead through the lens of faith. How big is your faith? It is your faith that connects you to God—*the God of the impossible* (Matt. 19:26).

Your finest hour is ahead of you. Nothing about your past, your environment, or your present circumstances defines you. No experience has the power to deter you, defeat you, or destroy you. Your life experiences up until this point have only happened to strengthen you—to show you what it is you don't want, don't need, and truly desire. Negative experiences may have scarred you or temporarily devastated you, but they cannot erase the fact that you are still here. I want to remind you that no matter what you have been through, you are not a victim. You are a visionary and a force to be reckoned with! Extraordinary is downloaded into your DNA. You are fearfully and wonderfully made (Ps. 139:14). Creativity and innovation were part of the intellectual repertoire given to you on the day of your conception. You may have lost touch with it, but writing your vision and daring to bring it to pass will reconnect you to your innate genius.

You have yet to experience your greatest moment. You would not be here now if your failures and setbacks were your defining moments. Remember, every setback is simply a setup for a

178

comeback. You are going to bounce back as you get your "grititude" back! Don't let your mind convince you those years are wasted years. There is nothing further from the truth. Visionary Nelson Mandela's defining moment did not come when he was arrested, nor did it come when he was imprisoned for twenty-seven years. It came when he chose to forgive and let go of all the hurts, hopelessness, and regrets. This simple shift redefined his life and reengineered the trajectory of an entire nation!

So say goodbye to your yesterdays and the hurts, betrayals, bondages, beatdowns, and discouragements that accompanied them. Yes, you may have had more than your share of bumps and bruises along the way, but nothing has defeated you! Your dreams may have been deferred and your vision frustrated, yet the truth remains: though delayed, they are not denied (Hab. 2:3). Your defining moment is on the way. It may come in the midst of your greatest personal challenge or a national catastrophe. No one gets a free pass out of the arena of life. We all have struggles, setbacks, and tragedies, but we are not our mistakes and misfortunes. You and I are here now with the power to shape our day and our future.

A FINAL CHARGE

You are a remarkable, most unique, wondrous, and magnificent specimen of God's creation—a one-of-a-kind phenomenon. There is no other you that has ever existed in the world. You will never be, nor can you ever be, duplicated or replicated. Don't live as a poor copy of someone else's life, an echo of someone else's opinion, a replica of someone else's expectation, or an imposter of someone else's purpose. God did not make you a poor copy of someone else, so refuse to live as if you are. Be you. You are an original. Decide to be the best version of yourself. Since God made you a sentient being, live life to its fullest by taking your mind out of neutral. You are the one who decides how you will live and who you will be. You will see in this world what you want to see, but when you change the way you look at the world and the way you see yourself in it, the world will change the way it looks—and in the process so will you.

God has appointed you to live in this generation and during this dispensation. Know for certain, He did not make a mistake. You are carrying something special this world needs. Not all of us have the same assignment, but when we all fulfill our own assignments, it is like putting together pieces of a puzzle. In order for the big picture to be complete, it takes common people doing uncommon things, ordinary people doing extraordinary things—everyone has his or her own assignment.

If you have thoughts that are contrary to the most elegant and amazing life you visualize, reject those thoughts immediately. Replace them with images that best represent your vision. Decree and declare what you expect to see manifested in the womb of tomorrow. When you have thoughts that are not in alignment with your ultimate vision of who you wish to become, what you want to have, where you want to live, and what you want to accomplish, quickly get rid of them by replacing them with who you do aspire to be, what you do want, where you do intend to go, and what you do hope to accomplish. When you say or do things that are misaligned with your highest aspirations and best intentions, make a pact with yourself and commit to never say or do so again.

Get rid of your emotional baggage. Learn the art of forgiving and forgetting. Forgetting is not the same as not remembering. Forgetting is the art of mentally, psychologically, and emotionally disconnecting with a certain reality. If others have offended you by their words or actions, forgive and emotionally disconnect from that reality as quickly as you can. This requires monitoring your thoughts, emotions, and actions until thinking, speaking, and acting in a positive, creative manner becomes a lifestyle.

Keep forward focused. "Keep your eyes straight ahead; ignore all sideshow distractions. Watch your step, and the road will stretch out smooth before you. Look neither right nor left" (Prov. 4:27, THE MESSAGE). (See also Joshua 1:7 and 23:6, and Isaiah 30:21.) Don't look at others' lives and believe for one moment that they are able to do more because they have more than you. We all have the same number of hours in the day. Use yours wisely. Rid yourself of the time wasters and the energy depleters, a.k.a. worry, doubt, and unhealthy competition. Managing what happens in your life and what comes to you starts with managing what flows through you!

Live in harmony with yourself. Speak kindly and lovingly to yourself. Make certain that your inner dialogue is aligned with your verbal declarations and affirmations. Don't sabotage your dreams by nursing old wounds or entertaining what could have been or what should not have happened. The last chapter of your life has not been written yet. "This is not the end. It is not even the beginning of the end, but it is, perhaps, the end of the beginning," said Churchill.[1] Therefore your past is only the introduction.

Today marks a new chapter of an amazing story yet to be told. You get to confer with God in deciding the theme, the players, and the outcomes. He will empower you to write your own story on the pages of your life. Make it a page-turner! Make it noteworthy! Make it newsworthy! Make it impossible to be ignored! Make it epic!

Give life all you've got. Commit to an action that moves you closer to the life of your dreams. Don't try it—do it. Do it now.

May you live your life in such a way that if it were a book, you would be a best seller. Live it passionately. Live it fearlessly. Live it boldly. Live your one precious life without regrets. This will only happen when you are able to say, "Goodbye, yesterday!"[2] and "Hello, tomorrow!"

> ...but this one thing I do, forgetting those things which are behind and reaching forward to those things which are ahead, I press toward the goal for the prize of the high calling of God in Christ Jesus.
>
> —PHILIPPIANS 3:13–14

- ◆ ◆ ◆ -

Declarations and Prayers

Throughout this book, especially in chapter 10, you learned about the power of words. There are no words more powerful than those from the Word of God. Use the following declarations to start harnessing the power of your words. Take time to look up the Scripture references, and boldly declare the truth about your life from God's Word as you sail toward your destiny.

Father, in the name of Jesus, I decree and declare:

Today I take 100 percent responsibility for my life—my success, failures, and accomplishments. I refuse to use other people or things beyond my control as reasons or excuses for not doing everything necessary to pursue my God-given vision and live the life of my dreams! I say goodbye to yesterday and hello to tomorrow!

My guiding principles for life and living are biblically based, values driven, socially impactful, interculturally appealing, and relevant to the times in which I live (Isa. 58:12).

I have clearly written down a description of my vision—my purpose and mission in life—and I am developing my gifts, abilities, talents, resources, networks, relationships, partnerships, and oppor tunities, as well as my confidence in who and whose I am and all I was meant to be, do, achieve, and accomplish (Hab. 2:2–3).

I arise today declaring your wisdom, favor, and grace over my day (Rom. 12:3–18).

This is a brand-new morning with brand-new mercies, brand-new opportunities, and brand-new strategies to seize every opportunity (Lam. 3:22–23; Isa. 43:19).

I decree this day a day of vision, inspiration, wisdom, and hope (Ps. 31:24).

This is the day You have made, and since everything You create has purpose, I am discovering, fulfilling, and manifesting my purpose today (Rom. 8:28; 2 Tim. 1:9).

This is the beginning of a new day. You have given me this day to use as I will. But nevertheless I say, not my will but Your will be done (Matt. 6:10).

I refuse to waste this day on maintaining the status quo—I will use this day for good. What I do today is important because I am exchanging my time for it. I want it to be gain, not loss; good, not evil; success, not failure—so that I will have no regrets (Rom. 14:12).

Today I choose to follow God's plans (Ps. 37:23).

Today nothing will disturb my peace (Phil. 4:7–11).

Today I will set my priorities and focus on the things that really matter (Matt. 6:33).

You are a good God, and therefore only good comes my way (Ps. 136:1–3).

I fully realize that no accomplishment, position, or amount of wealth can long endure unless built upon truth, authenticity, integrity, justice, and love as demonstrated in the Word of God; therefore I do not engage in anything that compromises these virtues. I do everything as unto the Lord (Col. 3:23).

I live in a world of unlimited potentiality and possibilities. I realize that in making decisions today, I also alter the realities of my tomorrow. With God all things are possible (Matt. 19:26; 2 Cor. 9:6).

I operate as a visionary thought leader (Prov. 29:18; Isa. 58:6–14).

I live a holy lifestyle that fosters peace, success, and prosperity (Heb. 12:14).

I decree victory in every challenge (1 Cor. 15:57; 1 John 5:4).

I resist every temptation to be slothful, for the hand of the diligent will rule (Prov. 12:24).

I live in a prosperous, healthy, beautiful environment (Ps. 16:6).

I am blessed even as I fulfill my purpose and assignment in the places You have planted me (Ps. 1:1–3; Deut. 28:3).

I face my greatest challenges, discouraging situations, and seemingly insurmountable problems with this resolution: "Only good can come out of this" (Gen. 50:20; Rom. 8:28).

I have great honor, respect, influence, and dignity (Deut. 28:10).

I live without limits, limitations, and lids (1 Chron. 4:10).

I pursue and invest in solid, mutually beneficial relationships (Prov. 13:20; Rom. 12:10; Eph. 5:1–2, 21).

I make the most of my time and every opportunity (Eph. 5:15–16).

I replace unhealthy habits with healthy ones (Rom. 12:1–2).

I deepen and live out my faith in God (Heb. 11:1, 6; Mark 11:24).

I pursue improvement, refinement, and upgrades in all areas of my life (Phil. 3:12).

I live morally and conduct all of my affairs ethically (2 Pet. 1:5–7).

I give my body the exercise, rest, and nutrition it needs (1 Cor. 6:19–20).

I see and experience improvements, refinements, and upgrades in all areas of my life so that every day and in every way I grow stronger and live with vibrant health. I nurture my soul (3 John 2).

I maximize my potential (Luke 13:6–9).

I value my spirituality and grow in the grace of the Lord (2 Pet. 3:18).

When I pray for answers, breakthroughs, opportunities, and divine intervention, rather than complaining while I wait, I will focus on gaining additional strategies for the actualization of my vision. I will use those precious moments as opportunities to prepare for my future, hone my skills, or help someone else do the same (Hab. 2:3).

Because a negative attitude toward others can never bring me success, I eliminate hatred, envy, jealousy, selfishness, indifference, pride, arrogance, unhealthy competition, negativity, criticism, and cynicism by developing love, the fruit of the Spirit, and compassion for all humanity (Gal. 5:22–23; 1 Pet. 3:8–17).

I succeed by attracting to myself the virtues, forces, and resources I wish to use, and I invite other people who work with me to do the same (2 Pet. 1:2–10).

I plan for and model generosity and give to those who can never reciprocate (2 Cor. 8; Deut. 15:10).

I walk in forgiveness toward others and myself (Col. 3:13).

I communicate with and care for my family (Gal. 5:22–23; 1 Cor. 13).

I do not make capricious promises. I do everything within my power to keep every promise and commitment I make (Matt. 12:37; Job 22:27–28).

I do at least one kind act each day for those who can never repay the favor (Prov. 19:17).

I declare peace within my mind and my relationships (Ps. 119:165; John 14:27; 2 Cor. 13:11).

I will not be trapped into believing that my place can be taken. I have no need to curse those who attempt to undermine my purpose. I choose instead to perceive them as individuals who desire to do more and to be more, even as I do, but lack the strategy to do it without fighting. I pray that they will find a strategy (James 1:2–4).

I overlook the inconveniences of the world and inconsiderateness of people because I know that whatever is beyond my control is under Your control, for my times are in Your hand (Ps. 31:15).

I run a very successful business because You are with me (Josh. 1:8; Ps. 107:23).

I leave a legacy for the next generation. Let my days speak and my years teach wisdom (Job 32:7).

I am diligent in earning and managing money, saving and investing more and spending less (Prov. 6:6; 13:22; Eccles. 11:1–2).

I am financially independent and live in the realm of success. I receive substantial return on my investments (Deut. 28:8).

I live in the realm of abundance. I have more than enough and overflow. My days of barrenness, lack, and struggle are over. My posterity and loved ones will never be homeless or beg for bread (Deut. 28:11; Ps. 37:25).

Everything that was lost, stolen, embezzled, sabotaged, undermined, hindered, diverted, or held up is released, restored, and redeemed with interest at the legal rate of no less than 10 percent compounded monthly, along with punitive damages and sanctions. I decree I will recover all with interest (Job 42:10–12). This includes:

- my health

- my peace

- my good name

- my stamina

- my wealth

- my business dealings

- my relationships

- my property

- my time

- my destiny

- my purpose

- my ministry

- my assignment

I will raise the bar on my expectations (Col. 3:1).

I use my mind wisely, creatively, and innovatively (Gen. 11:6; Prov. 8:12; James 1:5).

Nothing that crosses my path—no personal, professional, spiritual, cultural, or social challenge or circumstance—affects my peace, calmness, or composure (Phil. 4:7).

What I start I will complete. There will be no fruitless, harassing, or distractive activities. There will be no delays, setbacks, legal maneuverings, or ex parte motions. I command them to cease and be rejected in the courts of heaven in Jesus' name (Ps. 91; Zech. 4:9; Isa. 66:8–9).

I confess, acknowledge, and receive my possession of spiritual keys of the kingdom and all legal rights, licenses, and duties in the courts of heaven, and I use them to bind the activities of the enemy and to loose my blessings (Matt. 18:18–19).

I believe Your final heavenly judicial decree is ordered. Now is come salvation and strength and the kingdom of our God and the power of His Christ, for the accuser of our brethren, who accused us before our God day and night, is cast down and disbarred. And we overcome him by the blood of the Lamb and by the word of our testimony (Dan. 7:9–27; Rev. 12:10–11).

In Jesus' name, I reinforce that:

I walk in the Spirit (Gal. 5:16, 25).

I walk the right path (Prov. 2:9).

I live, walk, and conduct my life by faith (2 Cor. 5:7; Heb. 10:38).

I ensure my actions and responses are governed by the Word of God (Deut. 12:28; Ps. 119).

I am true to my convictions and core values (Matt. 16:26).

I feed my spirit (Jer. 15:16; 1 Pet. 2:2–3).

I hone my skills (Exod. 31:3–5).

I do not grow weary in doing good as I trust God to sustain me (Gal. 6:9; 2 Thess. 3:13).

I live authentically (1 Chron. 29:14–19; Matt. 5:43–47; John 1:19–23).

I do not waste time, but I order my affairs with urgency (Ps. 90:12).

I live a life of gratitude (Eph. 5:20).

I honor my word (James 5:12).

I properly manage my resources, time, habits, gifts, talents, relationships, finances, and opportunities (Prov. 27:23–27).

I am immune to fear and blind to any possibility of failure (Deut. 20:3–4).

I walk in total dependency upon You because I am conscious that the power in me does not emanate from me (Eph. 1:18–20; 1 John 4:4).

I realize I cannot embrace what You have for me in my future until I let go of my past (Phil. 3:13–14).

I commit my life, my vision, and all my endeavors to You, O Lord (Ps. 37:5).

I do my part in making this world a better place (Mark 16:15–18; Isa. 61:1).

I choose life and blessing (Deut. 30:19).

I refuse to live defeated, discouraged, depressed, or disillusioned. I decree peace is within the walls of my house and within my borders (Ps. 122:7; 147:14).

I choose to face every day with deliberate action based on my faith, my values, my passion, and my vision for making this world a better place (Ps. 25:12).

I choose (Deut. 30:19):

- life over death
- blessings over curses
- abundance over scarcity
- success over failure
- humility over pride
- serving over being served
- honor over dishonor
- truth over lies
- transparency over deception
- openness over closed-mindedness
- integrity over duplicity
- righteous living over unrighteousness
- character over compromise

- trust over distrust

- love over hate

- peace and harmony over conflict and war

- giving over receiving

- faith over disbelief

- courage over fear

- progress over stagnation

- prosperity over poverty

- health over sickness

- kindness over coldheartedness

- generosity over stinginess

- joy over depression

- diligence over laziness

- focus over distraction

- honesty over dishonesty

- morality over immorality

- loyalty over disloyalty

- faithfulness over betrayal

I choose patience. I will be anxious for nothing (Phil. 4:6).

I will let patience have its perfect work that I may be complete, lacking nothing (James 1:4).

I will elevate my expectations (Ps. 62:5; Eph. 3:20).

I maintain a prayerful attitude (Eph. 6:18; 1 Thess. 5:17).

I practice healthy, positive, successful, and prosperous thinking (Phil. 4:8; Josh. 1:8–9).

I renew my mind, and I have the mind of Christ. I have a positive mental attitude (Rom. 12:2; 1 Cor. 2:16).

I seek the wisdom of God before I make any decision (Prov. 3:5–6).

I know my mind-set determines my progress and success, so today I choose to think on whatever things are true, honest, just, pure, lovely, and of good report; if there is any virtue and anything praiseworthy, I think on these things (Phil. 4:8).

I meditate on Your Word until it becomes the source of all my inspiration (Job 32:8; 2 Tim. 3:16–17).

I choose to live a life that is dynamic. I refuse to blame others. I do not use others for selfish gain or as excuses for the choices I make. I make my own decisions, and therefore I choose to discard what does not work for me. I choose to rely less on others and more on the Holy Spirit (Gal. 6:7).

I communicate with honesty and act with integrity (Eph. 4:25).

I diligently love and care for my family (1 Tim. 5:8).

I am willing to serve others and the world, and others are willing to serve me (Luke 22:26).

I am cultivating a respectful attitude toward all human beings (James 2:1–10).

Lord Jesus, I trust in You. You have given me a great work to do. I acknowledge that You are supreme over all. You are the owner of heaven and earth. As a mere steward over a portion of Your creation, I know You are working on my behalf (Phil. 2:13).

Father, I pray:

Let Your Spirit rest upon me, the Spirit of wisdom and understanding, the Spirit of counsel and might, the Spirit of knowledge and the fear of the Lord. Let me not judge anything or anyone by appearance nor make a decision based on hearsay (Isa. 11:2–3).

Thank You, Lord, for choosing me. Thank You for anointing me. Thank You for pursuing me. Thank You for undergirding me. Thank You for empowering me. Thank You for keeping me. Thank You for blessing me. Thank You for prospering me. Thank You for watching over me (Eph. 5:20).

God, I give You permission to order my steps today. Teach me to trust You when I cannot trace You (Prov. 3:5–6).

Protect me from unrighteous ventures, vultures, and wolves in sheep's clothing (Matt. 7:15).

Remove anyone who distracts me from fulfilling my vision, discourages me, or undermines my vision (Gen. 13:14).

Bring those who are assigned to support me in the fulfillment of my vision into my life now (2 Chron. 2:1–18).

You are a strategic God, and You are no respecter of persons (Acts 10:34). I pray You will give me strategies to help me in every situation I face as I pursue the vision You have given me, just as You gave:

- Isaac a strategy to prosper in the midst of economic recession (Gen. 26:12–14)

- Jacob a strategy to leave an ill-paying job to become a successful entrepreneur and businessman (Gen. 30)

- Joseph an economic and wealth-creation strategy that changed the destiny of a nation (Gen. 41)

- Gideon a strategy to utilize insufficient military resources to win a battle over a military force that outnumbered his battalion (Judg. 7)

- Joshua a strategy to bring down the impenetrable walls of Jericho (Josh. 6)

- Moses an emancipation strategy to deliver his people from Pharaoh (Exod. 3–12)

- Elisha a community development strategy to heal the water supply (2 Kings 2:19–22)

- A widow a debt-reduction and wealth-creation strategy (2 Kings 4:1–7)

- Nehemiah a social reconstruction strategy (Neh. 1–6)

- Jael a warfare strategy (Judg. 4:17–24)

- Elijah a strategy to deliver his people from satanic strongholds operating through Jezebel (1 Kings 18:17–46)

- Daniel a strategy to rule in Babylon (Dan. 1–2)

Teach me to govern my actions according to vision (Prov. 29:18).

Sharpen my focus (Gen. 13:14–17).

Rid me of small-mindedness. Let me think bigger. Give me an outside-of-the-box mentality (1 Chron. 4:10).

Renew and revive my creative and innovative abilities (Exod. 35:31–32).

Give me the spiritual, emotional, and mental power to resist giving up or giving in to my emotions. You have not given me the spirit of fear, but of power and of love and of a sound mind (2 Tim. 1:7).

I ask You for wisdom to handle all important issues based on priority (James 1:5).

Every decision I make, every step I take, every action I engage in, every word I speak, and every thought I think is affecting my tomorrow. So teach me to number my days, to apply my heart to wisdom, and with this wisdom to make wise decisions (Ps. 90:12; Matt. 12:33–37).

- Help me not squander time, money, networks, or any resource given to me to succeed.

- Grant me the strength and wisdom to face my greatest challenges, anxieties, and fears with

> courage and conviction that I can overcome them all.

- Help me display courage and integrity and live a life of credibility at all times.

- Make me sharp in insight and quick in discernment.

- Let me see the opportunity hidden within every obstacle.

Let me live in faith and without fear. I take refuge in knowing that I am protected by You, Lord. You are my strength and protection (Ps. 91; Jer. 16:19).

Bless the month that lies ahead of me. Empower me to abound in every good work (2 Cor. 9:8).

Give me the grace to face my greatest challenge (Rom. 5:20).

Let me be steadfast, immovable, and unshakable in all things and in all situations (1 Cor. 15:58).

I thank You, Lord, for preparing and equipping me for the greater works (John 14:12).

Thank You for the presence of Your Holy Spirit, the greatest empowerment specialist, who enlightens me concerning my future (John 16:13).

I yield myself to Your guidance (Ps. 73:24).

I cast my cares upon You because You care for me (1 Pet. 5:7).

Help me govern my time according to Your revealed will for my life (Rom. 8:27).

Thank You for empowering me and strengthening me to accomplish every goal attached to the divine vision You have given me (Deut. 8:18; 1 Pet. 5:10).

Help me discern Your will and determine my times and seasons (1 Chron. 12:32; Eccles. 3:1).

Let me not covet what belongs to someone else (Exod. 20:17; Rom. 13:9).

I yield my desires and will to You, Lord. You give me the desires of my heart (Ps. 37:4).

Lord God, on a daily basis give me grace to accomplish every task and assignment divinely given to me (Ps. 84:11; Heb. 4:16).

Lord, according to Your Word, I declare:

You are my portion; therefore I hope in You (Lam. 3:24).

Lord, You are my strength and shield. My heart trusts You, and I am helped (Ps. 28:7).

Anything I do or accomplish is not by my might or by my power but by Your Spirit (Zech. 4:6).

You have given me power to prevail (Matt. 16:18).

You bless the works of my hands (Deut. 28:12).

Let Your Word dwell richly in me in all wisdom (Col. 3:16).

I know the thoughts You think toward me are good and that all things work together for my good (Jer. 29:11; Rom. 8:28).

Even youths faint and are weary, and young men utterly fall, but I wait upon the Lord. I renew my strength; I mount up with wings as eagles. I run and do not grow weary; I walk and do not faint (Isa. 40:30–31).

The Spirit Himself bears witness with my spirit that I am a child of God, and if a child, then an heir—an heir of God and a joint heir with Christ, if indeed I suffer with Him, that we may also be glorified together. For I consider that the sufferings of this present time are not worthy to be compared with the glory which shall be revealed in me (Rom. 8:16–18).

I stand fast in the liberty by which Christ made me free (Gal. 5:1).

There is surely a future hope for me, and my hope will not be cut off (Prov. 23:18).

I bring every thought into captivity to the obedience of Christ (2 Cor. 10:5).

I can do all things through Christ who strengthens me (Phil. 4:13).

I am fully convinced that what God promised He is able to perform (Rom. 4:21).

Now to Him who is able to do exceedingly abundantly above all that I ask or think, according to the power that works in me, to Him be glory in the church by Christ Jesus to all generations, forever and ever (Eph. 3:20–21).

For Yours is the kingdom and the power and the glory forever. Amen (Matt. 6:13).

NOTES

◆ ◆ ◆

INTRODUCTION

1. Adriana Cavarero, *For More Than One Voice* (Stanford, CA: Stanford University Press, 2005), 169, https://books.google.com /books?id=h9wuujvz1AsC&dq.

2. Online Etymology Dictionary, s.v. "voice," accessed May 3, 2018, https://www.etymonline.com/word/voice.

3. *Oxford English Dictionary*, s.v. "voice," accessed May 3, 2018, https://en.oxforddictionaries.com/definition/us/voice.

4. Online Etymology Dictionary, s.v. "hallo," accessed May 3, 2018, https://www.etymonline.com/word/hallo; Online Etymology Dictionary, s.v. "hello," accessed May 3, 2018, https:// www.etymonline.com/word/hello.

5. Jim Rohn, "Jim Rohn Personal Development Seminar," YouTube video, posted by "Documentary youtube," February 7, 2016, https://www.youtube.com/watch?v=jnBdNkkceZw.

6. Jim Rohn, as quoted on The Business Quotes, accessed May 11, 2018, http://www.thebusinessquotes.com/jim-rohn -quotes/.

7. Benjamin Disraeli, *Endymion* (New York: D. Appleton and Company, 1880), 117, https://books.google.com /books?id=GLglAAAAMAAJ&q.

8. Dr. Seuss, *Oh, the Places You'll Go!* (New York: Random House, 1960).

CHAPTER ONE: IT'S YOUR FUTURE—OWN IT!

1.   Nick Hoffman, "What's in a Name: Kettering Health Network," Cox Media Group, updated December 3, 2014, https://www.dayton.com/news/special-reports/what-name-kettering-health-network/Q8O8ZWrgXivtFQxWmUAB6K/.

2.   Garson O'Toole, "Whether You Believe You Can Do a Thing or Not, You Are Right," Quote Investigator, February 3, 2015, https://quoteinvestigator.com/2015/02/03/you-can/.

3.   Robert Collier, *Riches Within Your Reach!* (New York: Penguin Group, 2009), https://books.google.com/books?id=Orc1pRyjI9kC&pg.

4.   Online Etymology Dictionary, s.v. "vision," accessed May 3, 2018, https://www.etymonline.com/word/vision.

5.   William Shakespeare, *Hamlet* Act I, Scene 3, http://www.gutenberg.org/files/1524/1524-h/1524-h.htm.

6.   See my books *The 40 Day Soul Fast* and *Reclaim Your Soul*.

7.   *Oxford English Dictionary*, s.v. "vision," accessed May 4, 2018, https://en.oxforddictionaries.com/definition/vision.

8.   Jack Canfield, "Secret to Success," YouTube video, posted by "YouAreCreators," December 12, 2012, https://www.youtube.com/watch?v=DC4SA_6FqG4.

9.   E. H. Lindley, "The New Frontier: Charge to the Class of 1932," speech, the University of Nebraska (Lincoln, NE, June 4, 1932).

10.   "Official Report of the One Hundred Sixty-Seventh Semi-annual General Conference of The Church of Jesus Christ of Latter-Day Saints," October 4–5, 1997, https://archive.org/stream/conferencereport1997sa/conferencereport1997sa_djvu.txt.

11.   Theodore Roosevelt, "The Strenuous Life," April 10, 1899, http://voicesofdemocracy.umd.edu/roosevelt-strenuous-life -1899-speech-text/.

12.   Matthew B. Ridgway, *Military Review*, XLVI, No. 10 (October 1966), 46, http://cgsc.contentdm.oclc.org/cdm/ref /collection/p124201coll1/id/634.

13.   Robert H. Schuller, *You Can Become the Person You Want to Be* (New York: Hawthorn Books, 1973), 11.

14.   John Mason, *Know Your Limits—Then Ignore Them* (Tulsa, OK: Insight Publishing Group, 1999), 9, https://books.google .com/books?id=Juumj0XpgBYC&pg.

CHAPTER TWO: LEAVE ORDINARY BEHIND

1.   Blue Letter Bible, s.v. "*Tso'ar*," accessed May 8, 2018, https://www.blueletterbible.org/lang/lexicon/lexicon .cfm?Strongs=H6820&t=KJV.

2.   Napoleon Hill, *Think and Grow Rich* (New York: Skyhorse Publishing, 2016), chapter 2, https://books.google.com /books?id=OVSJCwAAQBAJ&q.

3.   See my book *History Maker*.

4.   Frederick Douglass, "My Escape From Slavery," *The Century Illustrated Magazine* 23, n.s. 1 (November 1881): 125–131, http://pagebypagebooks.com/Frederick_Douglass/My_Escape _From_Slavery/My_Escape_From_Slavery_p4.html.

5.   Ben Carson, interview with Kim Lawton, *Religion & Ethics Newsweekly*, January 11, 2008, http://www.pbs.org/wnet /religionandethics/2008/01/11/january-11-2008-dr-ben-carson -extended-interview/4847/.

6.   "Times Call for Liberal Action, Says Kennedy," *Lodi News-Sentinel*, May 13, 1961, https://news.google.com/newspapers?id

=QOgzAAAAIBAJ&sjid=g4HAAAAIBAJ&dq=americans+for+
democratic+action&pg=7056,2944411&safe=strict&hl=en.

7. Herodotus, *The Histories*, Book 7, trans. A. D. Godley
(Cambridge, MA: Harvard University Press, 1920), http://www
.perseus.tufts.edu/hopper/text?doc=Perseus%3Atext%3A1999.01.0
126%3Abook%3D7&force=y.

8. Robert Fritz, *The Path of Least Resistance* (New York:
Random House, 1989), 166, https://books.google.com
/books?id=z89m_l-XsV4C&q.

9. Bible Study Tools, s.v. "*apokalupto*," accessed May 8, 2018,
https://www.biblestudytools.com/lexicons/greek/nas/apokalupto
.html.

10. T. S. Eliot, preface to *Transit of Venus: Poems*, Harry
Crosby, in *Collected Poems of Harry Crosby*, comp. Caresse Crosby
(Paris: Black Sun Press, 1931), ix.

CHAPTER THREE: SET YOUR COURSE TOWARD TOMORROW

1. Antoine de Saint-Exupéry, *Flight to Arras* (New York:
Harcourt Brace, 1942), 129, https://www.amazon.com/Flight
-Arras-Antoine-Saint-Exupéry/dp/0156318806.

2. Stephen R. Covey, *The 7 Habits of Highly Effective People*
(New York: Free Press, 2004), 98, https://www.amazon.com
/Habits-Highly-Effective-People-Powerful/dp/0743269519.

3. "Tomorrow," The Doghouse Diaries, March 11, 2012,
http://thedoghousediaries.com/3474.

4. Darren Hardy, "Darren Daily," March 9, 2018.

5. Guadalupe de la Mata, "How to Promote Positive Change
in Teams and Organizations With Appreciative Inquiry,"
Innovation for Social Change, September 21, 2014, http://

innovationforsocialchange.org/social-innovation-methodologies
-appreciative-inquiry-problems-strengths/?lang=en.

6. "Generic Processes of Appreciative Inquiry," The Center for
Appreciative Inquiry, accessed May 4, 2018, https://www
.centerforappreciativeinquiry.net/more-on-ai/the-generic
-processes-of-appreciative-inquiry.

7. Brett Steenbarger, "Appreciative Inquiry: Leading by
Asking the Right Questions," *Forbes*, June 21, 2015, https://www
.forbes.com/sites/brettsteenbarger/2015/06/21/appreciative
-inquiry-leading-by-asking-the-right-questions/#580b3d432b53.

8. Marc Chernoff, "5 Things You Should Know About Letting Go," *Marc & Angel Hack Life* (blog), September 2, 2013,
http://www.marcandangel.com/2013/09/02/5-things-you-should
-know-about-letting-go/.

9. Howard Thurman, as quoted in "Howard Thurman Center
for Common Ground," Boston University, accessed May 9, 2018,
https://www.bu.edu/thurman/about/history/.

10. See my book *Prevail*.

11. Richard Paul Evans, *The Four Doors* (New York: Simon &
Schuster, 2013), 98, https://books.google.com
/books?id=TdWbAQAAQBAJ&pg.

CHAPTER FOUR: DARE TO DREAM

1. Michaela DePrince and Elaine DePrince, *Taking Flight*
(New York: Ember, 2014), https://books.google.com
/books?id=AMXaCwAAQBAJ&pg; William Kremer, "Michaela
DePrince: The War Orphan Who Became a Ballerina," *BBC
Magazine*, October 15, 2012, http://www.bbc.com/news
/magazine-19600296; David Smith, "Sierra Leone War Orphan
Returns to Africa En Pointe for Ballet Debut," *Guardian*, July 16,

2012, https://www.theguardian.com/stage/2012/jul/16/sierra
-leone-ballet-mchaela-deprince.

2. Marsha Sinetar, *To Build the Life You Want, Create the Work You Love* (New York: St. Martin's Press, 1995), 73, https://books.google.com/books?id=wicjIwzilFYC&pg.

3. Wikiquote, s.v. "Mark Twain," accessed June 1, 2018, https://en.wikiquote.org/wiki/Talk:Mark_Twain.

4. Napoleon Hill, *The Law of Success in Sixteen Lessons* (Blacksburg, VA: Wilder Publications, 2011), 388, https://www.amazon.com/dp/1617201782/ref=rdr_ext_tmb.

5. Hill, *Think and Grow Rich* (New York: Fawcett Crest, 1983), 15, 132, https://books.google.com/books?id=wr3lCEKeuXAC&.

6. Collier, *Riches Within Your Reach!*

7. Wikipedia, "Hero's Journey," last edited April 29, 2018, https://en.wikipedia.org/wiki/Hero%27s_journey#cite_note
-monomyth-website-1.

8. Joseph Campbell, *The Hero With a Thousand Faces* (Novato, CA: New World Library, 2008), 23, https://books.google.com/books?id=I1uFuXlvFgMC&q.

9. Campbell, *The Hero With a Thousand Faces*, 28–29.

10. Christopher Vogler, *The Writer's Journey: Mythic Structure for Writers* (Studio City, CA: Michael Wiese Productions, 1998), https://books.google.com/books?id=Lgzk7ElImugC&focus.

11. Donald Miller, *Building a StoryBrand* (New York: Harper-Collins Leadership, 2017), https://www.amazon.com/dp/B06XFJ2JGR/ref=rdr_kindle_ext_tmb.

12. "Storyline Conference Encourages Registrants to Live a Meaningful Narrative," May 10, 2012, Belmont University

News, http://news.belmont.edu/donald-millers-storyline
-conference-brings-special-guests-to-campus/.

13. "About Us," Groundworks Initiatives, accessed May 10,
2018, http://groundworksonline.com/about/; Ken Janke, "Story
Lab: A New Training Initiative...," *Social Innovators* (blog), June
10, 2010, https://socialinnovators.wordpress.com/2010/06/10
/story-lab-a-new-training-initiative/.

14. Ken Janke, "Story Lab: A New Training Initiative..."

15. Laura Buffington, "The Object of Desire," *Post Script*
(blog), June 6–7, 2010, http://www.southbrook.org/blogs
/postscript/theobjectofdesire6672010.html.

16. John Eldredge, *Desire: The Journey We Must Take to Find
the Life God Offers* (Nashville: Thomas Nelson Publishers, 2000),
11, 13, https://books.google.com/books?id=Xk-kbCTCT_UC&q.

17. Eldredge, *Desire*, 11, 13.

18. Leah Jessen, "One-Time War Orphan Michaela
DePrince Stars as Dancer With Dutch National Ballet Company," Daily Signal, August 21, 2015, https://www.dailysignal
.com/2015/08/21/one-time-war-orphan-michaela-deprince-stars
-as-dancer-with-dutch-national-ballet-company/.

19. *MacMillan Dictionary*, s.v. "desire," accessed May 10, 2018,
https://www.macmillandictionary.com/us/dictionary/american
/desire_1#desire_1__1.

20. Online Etymology Dictionary, s.v. "desire," accessed May
10, 2018, https://www.etymonline.com/word/desire.

21. Napoleon Hill, *Think and Grow Rich* (New York: Fawcett
Crest, 1983), 1, https://books.google.com/books?id=wr3lCEKeuXAC&.

22. Hill, *Think and Grow Rich*, 2.

23. Hill, *Think and Grow Rich*, 3.

24.   If you've not yet read *Think and Grow Rich*, you'll want to add it to your library, along with the precursor to this book, *Commanding Your Morning*.

25.   Hill, *Think and Grow Rich*, 17.

26.   Christine Caine, as quoted on https://www.pinterest.com /pin/438186238723117095.

27.   Wendy Farley, *The Wounding and Healing of Desire* (Louisville, KY: Westminster John Knox Press, 2005), 16, https://books .google.com/books?id=VrdeF6sVP7gC&q.

28.   As quoted on Dictionary Quotes, accessed May 10, 2018, http://www.dictionaryquotes.com/quotations/quotes-463.php.

29.   Charlena Ortiz, "How to Make the Right Decision," email sent from www.gritandvirtue.com, April 4, 2018.

CHAPTER FIVE: REIMAGINE YOUR FUTURE

1.   Kristen Butler, "In South Korea, 'Invisible' Tower Infinity Will Be an 'Anti-Tower,'" UPI.com, September 13, 2013, https:// www.upi.com/Odd_News/2013/09/13/In-South-Korea-invisible -Tower-Infinity-will-be-an-anti-tower/9331379078874/.

2.   Maxine Nwaneri, "When Tomorrow Becomes Today, Will You Be Ready?" *Success*, October 28, 2017, https://www.success .com/article/when-tomorrow-becomes-today-will-you-be-ready.

3.   Portions of this section were adapted from *PUSH*. Used with permission of Destiny Image.

4.   Daniel Gilbert, *Stumbling on Happiness* (Toronto, CA: Random House, 2006), 5.

5.   Online Etymology Dictionary, s.v. "imagine," accessed May 10, 2018, https://www.etymonline.com/search?q=imagine.

6.   Ian Wilson, "The Practical Power of Vision," *On the Horizon*, 1996, 4(2), 1, 3–5.

7. Myles Munroe, *Purpose for Living* (Shippensburg, PA: Destiny Image, 2011), https://books.google.com /books?id=VKnTmoSwJ0AC&pg/.

8. Munroe, *Purpose for Living.*

9. Myles Munroe, *Uncover Your Potential* (Shippensburg, PA: Destiny Image, 2012), 10, https://books.google.com /books?id=mD21_H7xbq0C.

10. Munroe, *Uncover Your Potential*, 11.

11. Hill, *Think and Grow Rich*, 11.

12. Marc and Angel Chernoff, "3 Things You Should Know About the Beliefs That Hold You Back," *Marc & Angel Hack Life* (blog), accessed April 5, 2018, http://www.marcandangel .com/2017/08/27/3-things-you-should-know-about-the-beliefs -that-hold-you-back.

13. Marc Chernoff, Angel Chernoff, *Getting Back to Happy* (New York: TarcherPerigree, 2018), 112, https://www.amazon .com/Getting-Back-Happy-Thoughts-Triumphs/dp/0143132776.

14. Marc and Angel Chernoff, "5 Things You Should Know About Letting Go," *Marc & Angel Hack Life* (blog), September 2, 2013, http://www.marcandangel.com/2013/09/02/5-things-you -should-know-about-letting-go/.

CHAPTER SIX: RENEW YOUR MIND

1. Caroline Leaf, *Switch On Your Brain: The Key to Peak Happiness, Thinking, and Health* (Ada, MI: Baker Books, 2013), 19, https://www.amazon.com/Switch-Your-Brain-Happiness -Thinking/dp/0801015707.

2. Leaf, *Switch On Your Brain*, 55–56.

3. Of note is the Neurosculpting Institute founded by Lisa Wimberger and the NeuroLeadership Institute founded by David Rock.

4. "The Medical Definition of Neuroplasticity," MedicineNet Inc., accessed June 4, 2018, https://www.medicinenet.com/script /main/art.asp?articlekey=40362.

5. Brian Tracy, as quoted on Jack Canfield's Facebook page, April 26, 2013, https://www.facebook.com/JackCanfieldFan /posts/10151396441665669.

6. Brian Tracy, as quoted on Jack Canfield's Facebook page.

7. Neville Goddard, *The Power of Awareness* (Seaside, OR: Rough Draft Printing, 2012), 13, https://www.amazon.com/The -Power-of-Awareness/dp/B00FK8J3VY.

8. Goddard, *The Power of Awareness*, 13.

9. Neville Goddard, *Prayer: The Art of Believing* (Altenmünste, Germany: Jazzybee Verlag, 2012), https://books.google .com/books?id=hUglgAbCIzMC&vq.

10. Bruce H. Lipton, *The Biology of Belief* (Carlsbad, CA: Hay House Publishers, 2008), xi, https://books.google.com /books?id=p6Pgi7b_ZCsC&q.

11. Lipton, *The Biology of Belief*, xxxi.

12. Hill, *Think and Grow Rich.*

13. Hill, *Think and Grow Rich*, 52–53.

14. Bruce H. Lipton, "Your perspective is always limited…," Facebook, July 10, 2013, https://www.facebook.com /BruceHLiptonPhD/posts/667704336577429.

15. Wikipedia, s.v. "darkness," accessed June 4, 2018, https:// en.wikipedia.org/wiki/Darkness.

16. Peter Baksa, "Can Our Brainwaves Affect Our Physical Reality?" The Huffington Post, November 11, 2011, https://www

.huffingtonpost.com/peter-baksa/-can-thoughts-manipulate
-_b_971869.html.

17.   Bruce Lipton, "The Wisdom of Your Cells," Mountain of Love Productions, accessed June 4, 2018, https://www.brucelipton .com/resource/article/the-wisdom-your-cells.

18.   James Allen, *As a Man Thinketh* (White Plains, NY: Peter Pauper Press, 1987), 13,16, https://books.google.com /books?id=1PRS3fY7pykC&vq.

19.   Tim Povtak, "Mind Over Matter? Yes, It's Working," *Orlando Sentinel*, August 28, 1988, http://articles.orlandosentinel .com/1988-08-28/news/0060320132_1_sports-psychologist -athletes-mental-imagery.

20.   Jack Canfield and Dave Andrews, *The 30-Day Sobriety Solution* (New York: Simon & Schuster, 2016), 237.

21.   Kirk Wilkinson, *The Happiness Factor: How to Be Happy No Matter What* (Austin, TX: Ovation Books, 2008), 100, https://books.google.com/books?id=X2aWVPyWYesC&.

22.   Marcus Aurelius, *Meditations*, XV, http://www.gutenberg .org/files/2680/2680-h/2680-h.htm

23.   Nikolas Tesla, *My Inventions: The Autobiography of Nikola Tesla* (New York: Experimenter Publishing Company, 1919), https://books.google.com/books?id=QdteCAAAQBAJ&.

24.   Charles W. Boatwright, "1973 Greater New Orleans Pro-am Open Invitational–Honoring Our Heroes, a True American Story!," *The QATSBY* (blog), April 26, 2016, http:// espygolfapp.com/blog/1973-greater-new-orleans-pro-am-open -invitational-honoring-our-heroes-a-true-american-story/.

25.   Collier, *Riches Within Your Reach!*

26. Jasmine Renner and Bowen Bailie, *Wisdom Keys to Releasing Your Creative Potential* (eBookIt, 2012), https://books.google.com/books?id=ysMp2cfa3sIC&pg.

27. Henry David Thoreau, *A Week on the Concord and Merrimack Rivers* (Concord River, MA: J. R. Osgood, 1873), 309, https://books.google.com/books?id=GtIgAAAAMAAJ&.

28. Goddard, *The Power of Awareness*, 23.

29. Goddard, *The Power of Awareness*, 24–25.

30. Goddard, *The Power of Awareness*, 20.

CHAPTER SEVEN: AWAKE TO YOUR DIVINE DESTINY

1. Jonathan Sandys and Wallace Henley, *God and Churchill: How the Great Leader's Sense of Divine Destiny Changed His Troubled World and Offers Hope for Ours* (Carol Stream, IL: 2015).

2. Jonathan Peterson, "God and Churchill: An Interview With Jonathan Sandys and Wallace Henley," Bible Gateway, October 7, 2015, https://www.biblegateway.com/blog/2015/10/god-churchill-an-interview-with-jonathan-sandys-and-wallace-henley/.

3. Peterson, "God and Churchill."

4. Peterson, "God and Churchill."

5. Douglas Russell, "On the Brink of the Abyss" (Winston Churchill in the Great War), WinstonChurchill.org, accessed June 4, 2018, https://winstonchurchill.org/publications/finest-hour/finest-hour-171/churchill-in-the-great-war-2/.

6. Winston Churchill, "Be Ye Men of Valour," BBC (first broadcast as prime minister, May 19, 1940), https://winstonchurchill.org/resources/speeches/1940-the-finest-hour/be-ye-men-of-valour/.

7.   Winston Churchill, "Never Give In" (speech at Harrow School, Oct. 29, 1941), https://winstonchurchill.org/resources/speeches/1941-1945-war-leader/never-give-in/.

8.   See "Invictus" by William Ernest Henley, https://www.poetryfoundation.org/poems/51642/invictus.

9.   John C. Maxwell, *Developing the Leader Within You* (Nashville: Thomas Nelson, 2012).

10.   "Malala Yousafzai," Biography, accessed June 3, 2018, https://www.biography.com/people/malala-yousafzai-21362253; Gordon Brown, "It's Up to Us to Deliver for Malala," The Huffington Post, October 15, 2012, https://www.huffingtonpost.com/gordon-brown/malala-yousafzai_b_1966409.html; Chelsea Clinton, "The 2013 Time 100," *Time*, April 18, 2013, http://time100.time.com/2013/04/18/time-100/slide/malala-yousafzai/; Gabrielle Giffords, "The 100 Most Influential People: Yousafzai," *Time*, April 23, 2014, http://time.com/collection-post/70822/malala-yousafzai-2014-time-100/; Mezon Almellehan, "The 100 Most Influential People: Malala Yousafzai," *Time,* April 16, 2015, http://time.com/collection-post/3822637/malala-yousafzai-2015-time-100/.

11.   *Meet the Robinsons*, directed by Stephen John Anderson (Hollywood: Walt Disney Pictures, 2007), DVD, end credits.

CHAPTER EIGHT: FIND YOUR LIFE COMPASS

1.   Wikipedia, s.v. "compass," accessed June 3, 2018, https://en.wikipedia.org/wiki/Compass.

2.   Visit KingdomU.net and TrimmCoaching.com to learn about courses and coaching.

3.   *Merriam-Webster*, s.v. "lodestone," accessed June 3, 2018, https://www.merriam-webster.com/dictionary/lodestone.

4.   John C. Maxwell, "Until I understand where I am…." Facebook, December 25, 2014, https://www.facebook.com /JohnCMaxwell/posts/10152854261772954:0.

5.   Idowu Koyenikan, *Wealth for All: Living a Life of Success at the Edge of Your Ability* (Raleigh, NC: Grandeur Touch LLC, 2016), https://www.amazon.com/Wealth-All-Living-Success -Ability/dp/0990639711.

6.   Buckminster Fuller, *Guinea Pig B* (Clayton, CA: Critical Path Publishing, 1983), 1, https://books.google.com/books?id =LSIsDwAAQBAJ&.

7.   Buckminster Fuller, *Synergetics: Explorations in the Geometry of Thinking* (New York: Macmillan Publishing, 1975), 298, https://books.google.com/books?id=AKDgDQAAQBAJ&pg.

8.   Wikipedia, s.v. "Degrees of Freedom," accessed June 3, 2018, https://en.wikipedia.org/wiki/Degrees_of_freedom _(physics_and_chemistry).

9.   Wikipedia, "Degrees of Freedom"; Fuller, *Synergetics*.

10.   Fuller, *Synergetics*.

11.   Greg Watson, "12 Degrees of Freedom," accessed April 16, 2018, http://12degreesoffreedom.org.

12.   Fuller, *Synergetics*, 297.

13.   Fuller, *Synergetics*, 224.

14.   Watson, "12 Degrees of Freedom."

15.   Max Lucado, *Let the Journey Begin* (Nashville: Thomas Nelson, 2015), 39, https://books.google.com/books?id =WCKMBQAAQBAJ&pg.

16.   Take the DiSC online survey, available at www.trimm international.com.

17.   Peter M. Senge, "The Leader's New Work: Building Learning Organizations," *Sloan Review*, Fall 1990, 9.

18. Senge, "The Leader's New Work."

19. W. S. Merwin, "The Estuary," accessed June 3, 2018, https://www.ablemuse.com/erato/showthread.php?t=267&styleid=1.

CHAPTER NINE: CREATE YOUR CANVAS

1. Jami Sell, *Thought and Belief: How to Unlock Your Potential and Fulfill Your Destiny* (Bloomington, IN: Author House, 2010), 60, https://books.google.com/books?id=U60TslRK7AcC&q.

2. Plato, *The Republic,* The Project Gutenberg, accessed June 3, 2018, https://www.gutenberg.org/files/1497/1497-h/1497-h.htm.

3. Aristotle, *Politics,* The Internet Classics Archive, accessed June 3, 2018, http://classics.mit.edu/Aristotle/politics.5.five.html.

4. *Oxford Dictionary,* s.v. "vision," accessed June 3, 2018, https://en.oxforddictionaries.com/definition/vision.

5. Tristan Loo, "How to Use a Vision Board to Activate the Law of Attraction," SelfGrowth.com, March 5, 2007, http://www.selfgrowth.com/articles/How_to_Use_a_Vision_Board_to_Activate_the_Law_of_Attraction.html.

6. Samuel Akinola Audifferen, *The Greatest Human Deception* (Maitland, FL: Xulon Press, 2006), 50, https://books.google.com/books?id=g0_EQfn6PJwC&q.

7. Loo, "How to Use a Vision Board to Activate the Law of Attraction."

8. Soledad O'Brien, "Prime Time With Soledad O'Brien," *Essence*, May 1, 2014, https://www.essence.com/2014/05/02/prime-time-soledad-obrien.

9. Loo, "How to Use a Vision Board to Activate the Law of Attraction."

CHAPTER TEN: VOICEPRINT YOUR VISION

1.   Ava Kofman, "Finding Your Voice," The Intercept, January 19, 2018, https://theintercept.com/2018/01/19/voice-recognition -technology-nsa/.

2.   Masaru Emoto, "What Is the Photograph of Frozen Water Crystals?" accessed June 3, 2018, http://www.masaru-emoto.net /english/water-crystal.html.

3.   Masaru Emoto, "What Is Hado?" accessed June 3, 2018, http://www.masaru-emoto.net/english/hado.html.

4.   See my book *History Maker* for more on this topic.

5.   Online Etymology Dictionary, s.v. "voice," accessed June 3, 2018, https://www.etymonline.com/word/voice.

6.   Online Etymology Dictionary, s.v. "invoke," accessed June 3, 2018, https://www.etymonline.com/word/invoke.

7.   *Merriam-Webster*, s.v. "sound," accessed June 3, 2018, https://www.merriam-webster.com/dictionary/sound.

8.   Brené Brown, "Courage Is a Heart Word (And a Family Affair), PBS, accessed June 3, 2018, http://www.pbs.org/parents /experts/archive/2010/11/courage-is-a-heart-word-and-a.html.

9.   Ben Kaplan, "Scenes From a Life: Bob Newhart," *National Post*, March 31, 2012, http://nationalpost.com/entertainment /scenes-from-a-life-bob-newhart.

10.   Lucy Handley, "How Jack Ma Built an Internet Giant," CNBC, November 1, 2017, https://www.cnbc.com/2017/11/01 /alibabas-jack-ma-on-e-commerce-in-china-globalization-and -trump.html.

11.   Sanjana Ray, "How Jack Ma Overcame His Greatest Failures to Become the Richest Man in China," YourStory, May 16, 2017, https://yourstory.com/2017/05/jack-ma-success-story-2/.

12.   Handley, "How Jack Ma Built an Internet Giant"; Liyan Chen, Ryan Mac, and Brian Solomon, "Alibaba Claims Title for Largest Global IPO Ever With Extra Share Sales," *Forbes*, September 22, 2014, https://www.forbes.com/sites /ryanmac/2014/09/22/alibaba-claims-title-for-largest-global-ipo -ever-with-extra-share-sales/; "The World's Billionaires," *Forbes*, 2018 rankings, accessed June 3, 2018, https://www.forbes.com /billionaires/list/#version:static.

13.   "Developing and Communicating a Vision," Community Tool Box (chapter 14, section 2), accessed June 3, 2018, https:// ctb.ku.edu/en/table-of-contents/leadership/leadership-functions /develop-and-communicate-vision/main.

14.   "Developing and Communicating a Vision," Community Tool Box.

15.   For more on this topic, refer to my book *Proclaim*.

16.   Wilferd Arlan Peterson, *The Art of Living, Day by Day* (New York: Simon & Schuster, 1972), 77.

17.   For more on this topic, refer to my best seller *Commanding Your Morning*.

CHAPTER ELEVEN: IGNITE YOUR DIVINE GENIUS

1.   See the Rules of Engagement books by Cindy Trimm, *The Art of War for Spiritual Battle*, *The Prayer Warrior's Way*, *When Kingdoms Clash*, and *'Til Heaven Invades Earth*.

2.   See *The 40 Day Soul Fast*, *Reclaim Your Soul*, and *The Prosperous Soul* by Cindy Trimm.

3.   Genesis 37 body head, NCV.

4.   Gina Amaro Rudan, *Practical Genius: A 5-Step Plan to Turn Your Talent and Passion Into Success* (New York: Simon &

Schuster, 2013), 19, https://books.google.com/books?id=Z-8Ec
-f8CZEC&q.

5.   Jonathan Fields, "Maker, Manager, and the 2% Challenge,"
The Good Life Project, Episode 284, August 26, 2015, http://
www.goodlifeproject.com/podcast/pick-your-two-percent-and
-put-everything-against-it/.

6.   See, for example, Stephen Covey, "Put First Things First,"
YouTube video, posted by "Coach Doh Motivation," accessed June
3, 2018, https://www.youtube.com/watch?v=ciBRcrOgFJU.

7.   Wikipedia, s.v. "Flow (Psychology)," accessed June 3, 2018,
https://en.wikipedia.org/wiki/Flow_(psychology).

8.   Alayna Kennedy, "Flow State: What It Is and How to
Achieve It," The Huffington Post, April 5, 2017, https://www
.huffingtonpost.com/alayna-kennedy/flow-state-what-it-is
-and_b_9607084.html.

9.   Michael Breus, *The Power of When* (New York: Little,
Brown & Co., 2016), https://www.amazon.com/dp/0316391263
/ref=rdr_ext_tmb.

10.   "What's Your Chronotype?" accessed June 3, 2018, https://
thepowerofwhenquiz.com.

11.   Daniel H. Pink, *When: The Scientific Secrets of Perfect
Timing* (New York: Riverhead Books, 2018), https://www.amazon
.com/When-Scientific-Secrets-Perfect-Timing/dp/0735210624.

12.   Jenna Goudreau, "14 Things Successful People Do First
Thing in the Morning," *Inc.*, accessed June 3, 2018, https://www
.inc.com/business-insider/14-things-successful-people-do-first
-thing-in-the-morning.html.

13.   Shawn Stevenson, "Get Financially Fit, Upgrade Your
Identity, and MAXOUT," *The Model Health Show*, episode 282,

accessed April 17, 2018, https://s3.us-east-2.amazonaws.com
/themodelhealthshow/Episode+282.pdf.

14. Stevenson, "Get Financially Fit, Upgrade Your Identity, and MAXOUT."

15. Stevenson, "Get Financially Fit, Upgrade Your Identity, and MAXOUT."

16. Stevenson, "Get Financially Fit, Upgrade Your Identity, and MAXOUT."

17. Jim Rohn, *Leading an Inspired Life* (Wheeling, IL: Nightingale-Conant, 1996), chapter 15, https://www.amazon .com/Leading-Inspired-Life-Jim-Rohn/dp/1555254594.

18. Robert Cooper (@RobertCooperPhD), "The first 22 minutes...," Twitter, December 14, 2015, 5:04 p.m., https://twitter .com/robertcooperphd/status/676523103082688513.

CHAPTER TWELVE: DISCOVER YOUR NEW FRONTIER

1. John F. Kennedy, "The New Frontier," acceptance speech, Democratic National Convention, July 15, 1960, http://www .americanrhetoric.com/speeches/jfk1960dnc.htm.

2. James McWhinney, "Understanding the Consumer Confidence Index," Investopedia, January 16, 2018, https://www .investopedia.com/articles/05/010604.asp.

3. Kennedy, "The New Frontier" (speech).

4. Kennedy, "The New Frontier" (speech).

5. Stevenson, "Get Financially Fit, Upgrade Your Identity, and MAXOUT."

6. My signature Executive Life Coaching program dedicates an entire unit to personal branding. Visit www.trimmcoaching .com to learn more.

7. Steven Pressfield, *Turning Pro: Tap Your Inner Power and Create Your Life's Work* (New York: Black Irish Books, 2012), https://books.google.com/books?id=FR7hAAAAQBAJ&printsec =frontcover#v=snippet&q=turning%20pro&f=false.

8. Online Etymology Dictionary, s.v. "entrepreneur," accessed June 3, 2018, https://www.etymonline.com/word/entrepreneur.

9. *Merriam-Webster*, s.v. "entrepreneur," accessed June 3, 2018, https://www.merriam-webster.com/dictionary/entrepreneur.

10. Brett Nelson, "The Real Definition of Entrepreneur—And Why It Matters," *Forbes*, June 5, 2012, https://www.forbes.com /sites/brettnelson/2012/06/05/the-real-definition-of-entrepreneur -and-why-it-matters/#70130bf74456.

11. Russell S. Sobel, "Entrepreneurship," The Concise Encyclopedia of Economics, accessed May 4, 2018, http://www .econlib.org/library/Enc/Entrepreneurship.html.

12. Eric Schurenberg, "What's an Entrepreneur? The Best Answer Ever," *Inc.*, January 9, 2012, https://www.inc.com/eric -schurenberg/the-best-definition-of-entepreneurship.html.

13. Barry Popik, "Conceive—Believe—Achieve," barrypopik .com, March 29, 2014, https://www.barrypopik.com/index.php /new_york_city/entry/conceive_believe_achieve/.

14. Robert K. Cooper, "What's the Most Exceptional Thing You've Done Today?," InnerSelf, https://innerself.com/content /living/finance-and-careers/career-and-success/7399-the-most -exceptional-thing-youve-done-today.html.

15. "Amygdala," Brain Made Simple, accessed June 3, 2018, http://brainmadesimple.com/amygdala.html.

16. Cooper, "What's the Most Exceptional Thing You've Done Today?"

17.   Cooper, "What's the Most Exceptional Thing You've Done Today?"

18.   Cooper, "What's the Most Exceptional Thing You've Done Today?"

19.   Robert Cooper, "Small Rules, Big Results," Upwire, episode 190, February 23, 2017, https://www.stitcher.com/podcast/upwire-hacking-human-nature/e/49236991?autoplay=true.

20.   Cooper, "What's the Most Exceptional Thing You've Done Today?"

21.   Cooper, "Small Rules, Big Results."

22.   See *Reclaim Your Soul* for more on this topic.

23.   As quoted in William J. Nippard, *The Leadership Ladder: 8 Steps to Maximum Success for You and Your Organization* (Nashville: WestBow Press, 2011), https://books.google.com/books?id=CFh9YSMhxTsC&pg.

24.   Kennedy, "The New Frontier" (speech).

EPILOGUE

1.   Winston Churchill, "The End of the Beginning," speech made at The Lord Mayor's Luncheon, Mansion House, November 10, 1942, http://www.churchill-society-london.org.uk/EndoBegn.html.

2.   Look for my forthcoming book *Goodbye, Yesterday!*

OTHER BOOKS BY CINDY TRIMM

Commanding Your Morning

Commanding Your Morning Daily Devotional

The Art of War for Spiritual Battle

The Prayer Warrior's Way

The Rules of Engagement

The Rules of Engagement for Overcoming Your Past

'Til Heaven Invades Earth

When Kingdoms Clash

KINGDOM™
SCHOOL OF MINISTRY

OTHER BOOKS BY CINDY TRIMM

Commanding Your Morning

Commanding Your Morning Daily Devotional

The Art of War for Spiritual Battle

The Prayer Warrior's Way

The Rules of Engagement

The Rules of Engagement for Overcoming Your Past

'Til Heaven Invades Earth

When Kingdoms Clash

KINGDOM™
SCHOOL OF MINISTRY